CANCER

Schmancer

Fran
Drescher

WARNER BOOKS

An AOL Time Warner Company

In this book, the identities of doctors, nurses, and others have been obscured or their names have been changed, including Vincenzo, Enid, Harriet, Tom, Sue, John, Marsha Rifkin, Richie, Lucy, Wanda, Marty, Yolanda, and Larry.

Warner Books, Inc., 1271 Avenue of the Americas, New York, NY 10020
Visit our Web site at www.twbookmark.com.

 An AOL Time Warner Company

Printed in the United States of America

First Printing: May 2002

10 9 8 7 6 5 4 3 2 1

ISBN: 0-446-53019-0
LCCN: 2002101586

Text design: Stanley S. Drate/Folio Graphics Co. Inc.

I dedicate this book to women with cancer,
those who lost the battle,
those who won,
and those who continue to fight.

Good health and good sense are two of life's greatest blessings.

—Publius Syrus (42 B.C.)

Acknowledgments

I thank the angels who guide me.
I bless the loved ones who support me.

All my gratitude and appreciation to:

My mother and father, who stood strong so that I could be weak.

My sister, who's not only an extremely smart nurse, but my life-long friend.

Elaine, my great friend, second mother, and brilliant manager.

Peter, who lovingly opened his heart, which meant the world to me.

Rachel, who defines the words *courage, intelligence,* and *friendship.*

My therapist, for setting me free.

Kathryn, the most loving, caring right arm a girl could ever hope for.

Howie, who's not only a devoted friend, but who also tirelessly edited and researched this book.

My surgeon, who saved my life and fights the good fight on behalf of women everywhere.

All the doctors and nurses who helped me and are committed to helping others each and every day.

Everyone at Warner Books who believed my story should be told.

And

John, the man I love, who valiantly and selflessly went to battle by my side and is now and forever my hero. His compassion and strength made all the difference.

Prologue

there I was in pre-op, awaiting my surgery. The makeup and hair team had done their usual best, natural and contemporary. The *60 Minutes* camera crew had created a surprisingly flattering light. Lesley Stahl was witty and sympathetic as we chatted about *The Nanny,* my career, and the projects I'd be working on next. After I recovered from surgery, of course.

As they began to put away their equipment, my dear friend Nicole Kidman stopped by to offer encouragement. Kissing me on the forehead, she slyly tucked a film treatment under my pillow. It was titled *Best Friends,* and she had her heart set on my costarring. What a doll! The project probably wouldn't ever happen, but just the fact that she'd thought of me meant so much.

While the orderly began to wheel me to the O.R. I thought, *He's not coming.* But then the hallway's double doors burst open and I heard the words, *"Stop! Wait!"*

"Brad, you came. You're so sweet," I said, noticing the stir Brad Pitt's presence was creating among the nurses. "I can't believe you came."

"Of course I came. You're having surgery, for God's sake," he responded, then kissed me softly on the lips. Wow, that was a first. And not bad, either.

"But what about Jennifer?" I asked, feeling like the other woman, more than a little embarrassed that this conversation was happening in public.

"That was a mistake, Fran," he replied. Then, leaning over, he whispered in my ear, "I love you."

"Oh, Brad, are you sure? Do you realize I have cancer?" I asked.

Fearlessly and eloquently, he responded, "Cancer schmancer!"

Boy, if only life were like the movies. . . .

The reality of the situation was quite different. Worried Jews (my family) were everywhere, crying, commiserating, and gorging themselves on Belgian chocolates. The nurse stuck stupid-looking blue hospital booties on my feet, which made me look like an oversize Smurf.

The orderly kept knocking my gurney around corners and through doorways like a drunk trying to drive through an obstacle course. There were no celebrities, no Lesley Stahl, and no cameras. In fact, in a vain attempt to keep my condition secret from the press, a towel had been placed over my face so I wouldn't be recognized. I was half comatose from the heavy sedation and wore a dopey grin on my face as drool dripped from my mouth. Definitely not the movies, but my life and welcome to it!

I thought of Donna, my dear old friend whom I'd met years ago on the film *Dr. Detroit*. She once took two days to tell her mom about a death in the family. I told her I couldn't believe how long she'd sat on the news. "Why?" she asked. "How would *you* have done it?"

Was she kiddin' me, or what? "With my family, if I walked into the room and said, 'Ma, I have something to tell you,' she would have screamed, 'Who died?' and in ten minutes half of Queens would have known." For me, life is loud, hearty, and full to the brim. Whatever I do, I do with gusto.

I was a chubby kid from Queens raised in a humble home by working-class parents. Somewhere along the line I moved to California, married my high-school sweetheart, got raped, became a famous TV star, divorced my high-school sweetheart, confronted my fears, lost the TV show, fell in love again, and got cancer. Whew! Whose life is that, anyway? I still can't believe it's mine. I didn't know I was going to write a book about the last couple of years, but this bout with cancer changed everything so profoundly I felt compelled to share my experience. I mean, if my last book—*Enter Whining*—was *Star Wars,* this, my friend, is *The Empire Strikes Back.*

Simply put, don't let what happened to me happen to you! I'm not a doctor (and no, I've never played one on TV, either), nor do I claim to have all the answers, but I do think you can learn from my experience.

Over a two-year period I saw seven different doctors in search of a diagnosis for my symptoms. I fell through the cracks every step of the way. It didn't matter that I was the Nanny and everyone loved the show. I didn't know what to ask for, and I wasn't offered all available tests that could have diagnosed me. So for two years I walked around with a progressively worsening cancer and none of these doctors, *not one,* offered me the simple test that ultimately detected it. Maybe they thought I was too young. Too young for uterine cancer, but just ripe for a perimenopausal hormone imbalance. Please, I could not accept I was beginning my menopause at the very moment I was single and entering my sexual peak! No way. And thank God I didn't, because nothing could have been further from the truth.

We need to educate ourselves about our bodies. Women need to understand gynecological cancers and the tests that can help detect them. We should know what's out there. We should hear our options. We should be in control. Once you wake up and smell the coffee, it's hard to go back to sleep! Let me sound the alarm. Since it's not my intention to point fingers at individual doctors, I don't name the names of those physicians I went to along the way. They're no different, no better, no worse, than the doctors you may encounter in your neck of the woods. It's not about *them,* it's about *you. Us.* We're the ones who must change, if we ever expect there to *be* change. We have to take control of the situation, become educated consumers, network among ourselves, and gain information and insight into getting diagnosed and getting treatment. Someone gimme a podium!

I've tried to be as honest as I can. Even my editor said, "Fran, I don't think we need to go into such detail about the change in your stool." *Nu?* I share my struggles, my pain, the knowledge I've gained, and the relationship I have with my boyfriend, who stood by me through it all.

If what follows impresses just one thing on you, I hope it's to never be passive when it comes to your health. Open a mouth! Assume that doctors, being human, are fallible, and remember that nobody knows your body as well as you do. Don't be an ostrich, either. A problem doesn't go away simply because you choose to ignore it. I promise you, the day will come when you can ignore it no more. And that's when the shit hits the fan. Trust me, early detection is crucial.

Although getting cancer was probably the worst thing that's ever happened to me (did I say "probably"?), there have been so many wonderful silver linings, too. Often, the truly great and valuable lessons we learn in life are learned through pain. That's why they call it "growing pains." It's all about yin and yang. And that's not something you order off column A at your local Chinese restaurant. They're the positives and negatives of life. One doesn't exist without the other. How you experience your pain, what you learn from it, and how you live through it—that's what makes all the difference.

This book is a celebration of life as much as anything. The joy and laughter I experienced with my family and friends, even during the worst of times, are the feelings I hope to leave you with. I definitely know more about women's medicine than I did before the cancer, but most important, I know my loved ones better, and I know how to live life more completely. That's my real triumph.

CANCER SCHMANCER

A Diagnosis

It seemed like any other day, but it wasn't. I was getting dressed to work out. Leesa, my exercise instructor, was already upstairs waiting for me. My housekeepers, Ramon and Angelica, a dear couple from Guadalajara who have worked in my home for years, were cleaning in the kitchen. My dog, Chester, was asleep on the bed. Then the phone rang. It was my gynecologist calling.

"Oh, hi," I said cheerfully.

"I got the results back from your tests. . . ."

"Yes?"

"I thought we should talk in my office, but then I figured calling would be easier than having you drive in and then having to drive home again," she rambled. I honestly didn't realize what she was getting at.

"It's okay," I told her, thinking I didn't want to drive in just to talk, either.

Then she said it. "You have adenocarcinoma. I'm very surprised myself."

"What's that?" I asked, still not really understanding.

"Uterine cancer."

I immediately burst into tears. She was saying I had cancer. *Me.* I got so scared. In that instant, my whole world came crashing down.

I'm going to die. This is it. My legs got so weak I dropped onto the bed. *I don't want to die. I don't want to be alone.* But I was alone with the phone to my ear. *This isn't me. There must be some mistake.* But it was me she was telling this to. Me, me, and only me. They were my tests that showed these results. *My body's turned on me. It's trying to destroy me. Dear God, why? What did I do? Did I do something to deserve this?*

Through my fears and tears the doctor got my attention. "Fran, it's in a very early stage. And uterine cancer is very slow growing and much less invasive than other women's cancers." As she spoke, I wrote everything down.

Nothing seemed to be working in my brain. I couldn't think, couldn't cognize this horror. I didn't know what to do. I began to panic. On *The Nanny,* whenever the shit hit the fan I'd wait a beat and then say, "Okay, here's what we're gonna do," and a whole plan would unfold. People would come to me for answers. But right in that moment I had no answers, no plan, no experience.

I was lost, like when I was a little kid and got lost in a crowd on a busy street. I didn't know where I was or how I'd get home. I couldn't find my parents. I was frightened, so very frightened. Sitting there, I was that little girl all over again.

"What happens now?" I asked.

"You'll need surgery, at least a partial hysterectomy," she answered. *A hyster-WHAT?* Growing up, my mom talked about relatives who'd had that surgery, and she said they were never the same after. That's what was always said: "She was never the same."

Oh my God, I don't want to become some kind of a freak. Will I still feel like a woman? Who will love me? Will anybody love me? A flood of questions ran through my head, but what came out were deep, guttural sobs.

"They *may* be able to save your ovaries. I don't know, that's up to the surgeon, so I've made you an appointment with a specialist. She's on the board at Cedars, considered one of the best nation-wide, and she's very compassionate."

My hand was shaking as I tried to write everything down. "When?" I asked.

"Friday. That's when she sees new patients."

This is only Monday, what do I do between now and then?

Just the week before, my mother had undergone a D&C for a polyp in her uterus and she was fine. No cancer, no hysterectomy, just a few snips on a benign growth as an outpatient and boom, good as new. That's what I'd been expecting, too. But she'd passed her test and I'd failed mine.

I have cancer? This doesn't make sense. I'm the strong one, the healthy one. Good peasant stock, that's what I'm made of! I took down the surgeon's number and address. She was in the cancer center at Cedars. *Cancer center? Where all those really sick people go?*

I suddenly thought about Peter, my ex-husband. The man I'd been with since I was fifteen. For more than half my life we were together. Husband and wife, coworkers, codependent friends. Un-til recently. Just recently when it all came apart, ending in a di-vorce. All those years, we'd trudged through thick and thin.

I remembered his parents, Pat and Eddie, both brought down in the prime of their lives by lung cancer. How they both went through chemo and radiation treatment. How they both suffered as their bodies slowly wasted away before they finally died. *I don't want to go that way. Dear God, I never want to go that way.*

The doctor said to call her if I needed anything. "Even if it's just for a hug," she added.

I thanked her, but I'm not sure why. Only a week earlier she'd assured me I didn't have cancer. She'd sat in her office and said, "Fran, you do *not* have cancer." Those were her exact words, and now all she could say to me was, "I'm very surprised"?

I hung up the phone feeling queasy. My stomach was in knots. If I'd eaten breakfast I'm sure I'd have vomited right then. This was misery of Gothic proportions. That one call became the marker by which my entire life would be divided in two. Before cancer and after.

In the Beginning

i think I need to start at the beginning of my whole health crisis and catch you up to the day I finally got diagnosed. I say "finally" because it took forever—more than two years and eight doctors—before one of them decided to give me a D&C, which stands for "dilatation and curettage," whatever the hell that is. Basically, it's when they scrape tissue from the uterus for biopsy. In the end, this was the only test I needed to find my cancer. Because I was atypical for contracting uterine cancer, at each turn in the road I kept being steered in the wrong direction.

Just when my life had moved into a new place, I began to experience symptoms. When I say "moved into a new place," I mean a place without Peter, my childhood sweetheart and husband for almost twenty years.

One of the hardest things, if not *the* hardest thing, I've ever done was leaving that man. For me it was like walking through fire, because I was never one to leave anything. I had trouble parting with our old '78 Buick, so leaving the person I'd been with since I was fifteen seemed impossible.

We had a beautiful home, wonderful friends, and together had created our single greatest achievement to date, *The Nanny*. But I was miserable. When you achieve everything you've ever dreamed of or wanted, and you're still unhappy, the time has come to stop looking without and start looking within. I'd agonized over this for years.

We'd begun to fall apart after the night we became victims of a violent crime, years before. That night was the night that changed everything. Two men with guns broke into our home. They were brothers on a rampage. While one loaded our car with all our valuables, the other, who was out on parole, tied Peter up and raped both me and my girlfriend Judi, who had the misfortune of having joined us for dinner.

I don't think we truly realized the impact that experience had on us, but in fact we were never the same again. If we were insecure about being apart from each other before the attack, afterward we were riddled with fears, suffocated by codependency. We imprisoned ourselves in our home, put bars on the windows and doors, purchased an elaborate security system, and couldn't make a move without looking over our shoulders. We lived with a heightened sense of danger all the time. We couldn't sit in our yard without the alarm's remote panic button. For years we continued to ignite fear in each other. I envied Judi, who got to leave the scene of the crime and live among normal people who weren't scarred by what happened that night.

I remember one afternoon we were taking a walk, in Beverly Hills no less, when a car pulled up alongside us to park. Peter grabbed my arm and we began racing in the opposite direction, imagining that these people were going to hold us up. And all they were doing was parking their car. Clearly, we were in trouble. And it was our marriage that paid the price.

It wasn't all bad, though. We had great times, happy times, and a deeply committed friendship. But marrying your high-school sweetheart, as romantic a notion as that sounds, is probably not the best idea. We were too young, too inexperienced with life, and underdeveloped as individuals. Even though we were extremely compatible in our humor, ethics, food, and art, our greatest compatibility was in how we complemented each other's neuroses.

He was a person of many needs and I needed to be needed. We both had a fear of being abandoned, and that kept each of us from leaving. I was completely out of touch with my own feelings, and he was consumed by his. We loved each other very much, he just had a lot of problems. And so did I. It wasn't until I went into therapy that I began to find some answers. And boy did I get an earful.

At the risk of sounding like a cliché, I needed to find myself. I didn't know who I was as a separate person from Peter. I realized I was a woman who had no opinions apart from my husband's, no identity outside of who I was in the relationship. I was completely codependent, incapable of buying a simple chair or garment without saying, "What do you think, honey?"

I never knew how to apologize to anyone for anything. Not one of my more flattering traits. On *The Nanny* I obsessively tried to track the trains that would lead me to who was really at fault when something went wrong, because I never wanted to be blamed for anything. I was the same way in my marriage.

Working on *The Nanny* was, in itself, a monumental undertaking. But doing it while my marriage was falling apart was a killer. Even now, I'm surprised Peter and I managed to pull it off each week. We always thought of the show as our baby, and no matter how hard things became in our personal lives, we tried not to bring them to work. The show must go on. We never missed a day of work. We never shut the show down. And in many ways it was our savior. There remained a real need to be civil to each other even during the hardest of times. That's not to say we never had fights backstage or screaming matches in our office, but they weren't the norm. Thank God.

Ya gotta understand, I never really wanted to leave Peter. I loved him, and he loved me. But I felt so trapped by my problems that despite my crippling fear of being alone, I left. It was after a terrible fight we had. I slept in the guest room. It was the last night I ever spent in our home. My dream house, I once called it. The next morning I checked into a hotel. I knew if I didn't escape, become my own person, and get over my fears once and for all, I wouldn't be happy with him or anybody. The first night I slept in a bed without him, my body twitched and shook from fear. It was *that* difficult.

Much to my horror, within forty-eight hours word reached the press that we were separated and all hell broke loose. In the middle of the night I got a call from my publicist saying she'd received a tip that the press knew where I was staying and that I had to get out. Reporters were also camped out on the front lawn of our house, where Peter was still living. It was a nightmare. I had never experienced anything like it. And needless to say, it exacerbated the situation tenfold. We were both so raw with pain, guilt, and regret, the last thing we needed was to be put under the tabloid spotlight.

Judi and my manager, Elaine, two of my best girlfriends whom I love dearly, helped me look at apartments out by the beach. Many people said the beach was very medicinal, and I needed all the medicinal I could get, so we all loaded into Elaine's Cadillac and headed west.

That afternoon I found a little one-bedroom right on the ocean. Afterward, the three of us had lunch at a nearby café. I remember Judi gabbing a mile a minute about how cute I could make the place, while Elaine went on and on about what a find an apartment with a sunset view and two parking spaces was. But there I sat, practically comatose, nauseous and in shock, chewing on a tuna sandwich. What was I doing? Letting myself out of the cage I'd put myself into many years before, that's what. So I did it, signed my name on the dotted line of a one-year lease.

It was far from what anyone would expect a famous sitcom star to live in, but for me it was perfect. I didn't want some large house with a lot of rooms. The thought of it scared me. I'd never lived on my own before, not once in forty years. I wanted to be able to see all the rooms as soon as I walked through the front door. I was living my life backwards. At twenty, I'd lived like a forty-year-old; at forty I was living like I was twenty.

The apartment had a living room, a terrace, a fireplace, a little kitchen, a little bedroom, and a little bathroom. I turned the bedroom into an office/dressing room and put my bed in the living room with the fireplace, terrace, and view, more like a great hotel suite than an apartment. I decorated it sparingly with overstuffed, upholstered pieces in shades of white, and picked up a few casual antique tables and dressers.

That sounds easier than it was. I remember one night lying in bed with my dog, Chester, having an anxiety attack over a rocking chair I'd bought from Shabby Chic. The fuss I made over that rocker made me realize I was literally off mine. It's so strange how riddled with contradictions I was. During the day, an executive producer of a hit television show, but at night a weeping baby.

I must admit, though, I was proud of the way the place looked when I was finished decorating. I was living alone, without bars on my windows. No matter what I'd achieved on *The Nanny,* being on my own in this tiny little apartment seemed my greatest accomplishment.

One step at a time. I was managing. Not easy, but definitely on the right path. Meanwhile, why was I experiencing strange bleeding and cramping in the middle of my cycle? The first couple of times it happened, I chalked it up to stress, but now it was becoming a regular occurrence. Still, it wasn't *a lot* of bleeding, and it wasn't like it was happening *every* day or anything. All I needed was a simple panty liner and I could easily ignore it. But it was becoming chronic, so after a few cycles I decided to call Doctor #1, the gynecologist I'd been seeing for years.

I sat in her examining room. As usual, I nervously dabbed a little Chanel No. 5 below my belly button. What? It shouldn't be a pleasant experience for the doctor? I glanced at the wall, which was covered with snapshots of all the babies my doctor had delivered. One kid in front of a Christmas tree had reindeer antlers on his head. The dog beside him wore a red suit and a beard like Santa. Well, I suppose it's better than the butt shot on the bearskin rug from my day.

Doctor #1 eventually breezed in and snapped on her gloves. I slid down to the table's edge, placing my heels in the stirrups. There was no mention of the perfume. I wondered if she was more a Shalimar gal.

I brought her up to date on my symptoms. "I keep experiencing this cramping in the middle of the month and after sex, like I'm about to get my period."

"Do you take anything to help relieve the pain?" she asked, while performing a relatively painless Pap smear. I knew there was a reason I preferred a female gynecologist. Small hands!

"I usually take an Advil and the cramps subside," I responded.

"Well, I wouldn't worry about anything a single Advil can take care of." She didn't seem very concerned, which was a relief, but I thought she did seem a bit hyper. She talked a mile a minute as her head periodically popped up from behind the paper sheet that draped across my thighs.

She brought up the Chinese herbs I knew she was selling on the side to Judi and a few of my other girlfriends to help them lose weight. *Oy.* I never liked the idea that my gyno was into that, too. I should have known then. "I've been taking them for two years now," she said, while pressing on my abdomen. "I'd like to stop, but I'm afraid I'll gain weight."

"What do you make of my midmonth staining?" I asked, while noticing on the wall a set of triplets dressed like bunnies.

"You're probably perimenopausal. It's the precursor to menopause and a common symptom in middle-aged women." *Middle-what?* "In France they consider it normal," she added.

My mind wandered as I began to obsess on Catherine Deneuve. Catherine Deneuve is French and she looks great. Does Catherine Deneuve stain between periods? Does Catherine Deneuve still get her period? Did Catherine Deneuve get a face-lift?

"Fran, what about having children?" Doctor #1 said, pulling me back into the moment. "Do you plan to? Because time is running out!" By this point she was annoying me. My life was so up in the air I had no idea what I was having for breakfast, let alone what I was doing about having kids. But the photo of that very fat, bald baby in his tiny baseball uniform sitting in a catcher's mitt sure looked cute.

In that moment I made a mental note to stop seeing a gynecologist who was also an obstetrician. I mean, I needed this pressure like a hole in the head. So I pulled up my pants and left with a sample bag of Chinese weight-loss herbs and a clean bill of health. I had cancer at the time.

Dating

Well, by the time the fifth season of *The Nanny* ended and our hiatus began, Peter and I, and the whole cast and crew, breathed a sigh of relief. We could escape from each other and all the pressure. Peter packed up and went to New York, while I stayed in L.A. We took separate coasts for that hiatus and spent the next months free from it all. It was during this period that I allowed myself to really feel single.

There I was, a forty-year-old woman, and I'd never really dated. I began to make new friends and branch out from the married couples Peter and I had known for years. This helped me discover who I was outside of the marriage. Somehow I fell in with a group of Europeans who were very social. They were always throwing parties, and I was always game to go.

For the first time, I felt like I could be whoever I wanted to be. Free to decide everything for myself, without feeling encumbered by my nagging inner voice always trying to do what was best for those around me. I was someone with no experience being on my own. Zilch! I never went away to college, never even went away to camp! At the age of nineteen I moved out of my bedroom in my parents' apartment in Queens and in with Peter. But now it was time to have some fun.

It's not that I was wild—God knows, nobody would ever describe me as that—but I was "open." I wanted to meet new circles of friends and I appreciated whenever I was included. I used to tell everyone, "I'm hard up, invite me!" I remember my English friend Kat, a well-known interior decorator whom I'd been friends with for years, was entertaining some Italians who were visiting L.A. We all decided to take a hike in the mountains together.

Well, one of the three men, Vincenzo, was so gorgeous. I mean, like right out of *La Dolce Vita*. Black wavy hair, dark sunglasses, and dazzling white teeth. He was olive-complected and dressed casually in whites and tans. He had an adorable Italian accent and spoke limited English. Perfecto!

There we were on the hike when Vincenzo and I started to hit it off. "I see *Nanny* in Italia," he said. "It call *La Tata*."

Smooth move, I thought. Talking about one of my favorite subjects.

"I like sound of you voice," he said.

Does he realize the show is dubbed in Italy?

"You much more beautiful and younger in person than TV."

Well, no language barrier here. Honey, come to Mama! By now I'm workin' my mojo, gettin' that whole thing goin', and I'm checkin' out his legs, his clothes, the way the tendrils of his hair spill over the white collar of his shirt, even his fingernails. And after careful inspection, I'm still interested.

After the hike we all wound up at a beachfront restaurant for margaritas and then at my apartment just to hang out for a while. Despite the place being so small, they all loved its white, airy look and felt very comfortable. One by one everybody had somewhere else to go. Everybody except Vincenzo, that is.

Now, remember, I was new to dating and not very experienced. Oh well, better late than never. I gotta admit, I was feeling a nervous flutter in my stomach when I closed that front door on the last visitor and turned back to the room to see Vincenzo sitting on my couch, arms spread across the back, smiling from ear to ear. That looked like an invitation if ever I'd seen one, and so I sat down next to him. Within moments we began making out. But where does "making out" end at this age when you've got your own pad and can no longer use your parents as an excuse to cut the evening short?

On the other hand, what was I worried about? If I wanted to, I could have sex with him. I could do whatever I wanted. I was a grown woman. But I was really a freak. With little or no sexual experience other than with my husband, I was literally feeling my way through.

I know it sounds weird, but my marriage to Peter had sheltered me from the mid-1970s through the mid-1990s. I was like Rip Van Winkle, sleeping right through the sexual revolution. I used to feel like a bore, always being part of an ol' married couple when the whole "Me Generation" was sleeping around. A therapist once told us we were "too young to be in such an old relationship." Well, it sounded good at the time, but actually nothing could have been farther from the truth. In reality, we were too old to be in such a young relationship. Both of us were emotionally immature, under-developed, and lacking insight.

Well, as beautiful as Vincenzo was, I can't say he was a very good kisser. I'm sorry, but for me the quality of the kiss means everything. *Oy*, it was all wrong. The mouth was too open, too much tongue, not enough lip. And then he started biting me! Can you believe that? Was this supposed to be sexy?

"Vincenzo, quit biting me," I said. "I wear very revealing clothes on *The Nanny* and I can't be getting bite marks!" A few things began racing through my mind: His friends left him without a car. I really didn't want to be doing this anymore, but what to do with him? Should I just sleep with him and get it over with? Or reject him, hurt his feelings, and then have to deal with him during that awkward waiting-for-the-taxi-to-arrive period?

Is that crazy? I mean, what a baby, what a dope I was, actually considering sleeping with a man who promised to be a lousy lover just to avoid making him feel bad. There was my problem staring me right in the face: To what lengths would I go, how much was I willing to sacrifice, just to make others happy?

Suddenly sanity took over and my inner voice said, *You don't want to go through with this? Don't!* And I heard myself saying, "This isn't going to happen, you have to go." Wow. I did it. And it took only forty years and a lotta therapy to get there. What was far more important to my growth than sleeping with Vincenzo was being able to tell him I wouldn't.

As the taxi arrived—thank God, in no time flat—I closed the door on Vincenzo, and felt like I'd turned a page in this chapter of my life.

The First Pilot for MTV

July 1998

the staining and cramping persisted, and it made me feel embarrassed and inadequate. If I truly was perimenopausal, as Doctor #1 suggested, that meant I was getting old. I hated that idea. Besides, didn't most women start this stuff in their fifties? At what age did it start for my mom? I called her to find out.

"Hello?"

"Ma, tell me something, when did you begin to experience the first signs of menopause?" I asked, while inspecting my hands for liver spots.

"Morty, turn off the teapot, the whistle's blowing!" she screamed. "He don't hear anymore, where was I?" she said as Oprah droned in the background.

"Menopause, when did it start for you?" I repeated, wondering if my body was aging at some weirdly accelerated rate.

"Why?" she asked.

"I don't know. The doctor's thinking maybe that's why I'm staining."

"A lot of women go through an early menopause. Do you get hot flashes?"

"Hot flashes? No way." Suddenly I felt nauseous. "Let's change the subject."

"Hmm. Did I tell you Grandma Yetta hung up on me when she tried to shut off the TV with the telephone? Is she funny, or what?" my mom asked.

"Hysterical," I answered. But I wasn't laughing.

Fate was playing a dirty trick on me, giving me an early menopause just when I was starting my life over again. I pictured myself getting night sweats and a lowered libido. I felt like damaged goods, imperfect.

So while I pretended to be the picture of health to the outside world, I secretly decided to see another gynecologist, Doctor #2. Leesa, my exercise instructor, had said he was really good, that he was doing all kinds of breakthrough hormone treatments in women's medicine. A magazine had even reported on his controversial, even radical, theories regarding the usage of natural thyroid and growth hormones to keep a woman in a perpetual state of youthfulness. I'll tell ya, that just don't sound kosher to me. I know there ain't no fountain of youth. But meanwhile, I went to see him anyway.

As I sat in the waiting room a young woman entered the office and asked at the desk for her pills. She seemed to be in her twenties, but she could have easily been in her thirties. Perhaps she recognized me, I don't know, but while she was waiting, she struck up a conversation.

"Is this your first time here?"

I nodded, slightly overwhelmed by her bouncing-off-the-walls energy.

"Let me tell you, he is a great doctor. A true genius," she said, talking a mile a minute. "Look at my skin! Look at my hair! I've never felt better in my whole life. And I'm not the only one, all my sisters go to him. We all take his hormone replacement regimen and we've never felt better or more energized!" *Calm down, honey, you're gonna explode!*

Sounded more like Scientology than gynecology, I thought, as the nurse showed me into the doctor's office. There, behind a large desk covered with bottles of pills, sat an older man with a foreign accent who wore clogs. He seemed very bullish on his arsenal of medications, but meanwhile he was still getting over the flu. So there you are.

Between sneezes and coughs, he questioned me about any family history of cancer. "There's none on my mother's side, but my dad's sister died from ovarian cancer," I said as I handed him a tissue. I remember saying with conviction, "I don't have cancer."

"I do extensive state-of-the-art blood tests," he said. "I'll need at least seventeen vials of blood, to be thorough."

"Seventeen vials?" I said, recoiling.

"They're *small* vials," he countered. "And we send them out of state for the best analysis." Where, Transylvania? Who *was* this guy?

In the meantime he talked about putting me on his program, which included the taking of a natural thyroid pill. I explained that I was already taking Synthroid medication for Hashimoto's disease, a very common thyroid condition. (Thyroiditis is the most common disease among women. It's hereditary, and all women should be tested for it by an endocrinologist.) It annoyed me that in this first visit he was already pushing pills.

His exam was pretty typical: stirrups, pelvic, and Pap. He couldn't do the blood test because it had to be done on a specific day of my cycle. I got dressed and left, but I never returned.

So I went back to taking my Advil and business as usual. It was right around this time that a sitcom script I'd written was green-lighted to become a pilot for MTV. This was my first real venture on my own apart from Peter and *The Nanny,* and I executive produced and directed it as well. The concept was a Gen-X *Odd Couple*. It was a massive undertaking, a real milestone for me.

As exhilarating as the experience was, it was also a rude awakening. I, who'd always had Peter by my side to support and console me after a long and hard day's work, now came back to an empty apartment. Too tired even to go out for dinner, I'd sit on my bed working on my camera shots by the light of my reading lamp, eating food my housekeeper Angelica had left in the fridge. At this point Peter and I were sharing Angelica and her husband, Ramon, depending on them to keep our places tidy. Some days they'd clean and cook for him, other days they'd do the same for me. I felt lonely, but kept trying to talk myself out of it. *This isn't a negative,* I'd tell myself. But old habits die hard, and as much as I tried to convince myself I was a successful single person enjoying the solitude of her beautiful home, the old tape of feeling like a lonely spinster-in-the-making kept looping though my brain. Still, I forged ahead. MTV was spending a lot of money for this pilot and, come hell or high water, I was going to rise to the occasion.

I surrounded myself with many of the same people I'd worked closely with on *The Nanny,* which made things easier. But since literally every decision rested on my shoulders, I found myself working harder than ever. The amount of stress I was feeling might have worsened my symptoms. After hours and hours of standing on the hard soundstage floors I was beginning to feel it in my lower abdomen. *Is this also part of getting older?* I thought, while taking some Advil and stealing moments to sit down in my director's chair.

It was on this project that I started to become friends with my associate producer, John, someone I'd also worked with on *The Nanny.* In all those years on the show, I can't recall having had a single conversation with him, but on the MTV pilot that all changed. I'd always found him easy on the eyes. There was a Mediterranean look to him that I found very attractive. He had long dark hair, deep brown eyes, and a winning smile. His features weren't pretty, but attractive in a more horsey, masculine way; *like Travolta,* I thought.

He was much younger than I. Sixteen years, to be exact. But I was working for MTV, and had intentionally surrounded myself with young people. And I, who in my head and heart was feeling young for the first time in my life, enjoyed hanging out with all the Gen-Xers. There was something about John's mild manner and laid-back attitude that appealed to me. I liked him, and with all the pressure I was feeling to do well, his became the calming energy I needed.

At first, except for occasional conversations about music we both liked, our involvement with each other was entirely work-related. This was my first time shooting in a single-camera format, and I needed someone watching the monitors to make sure I'd shot all I needed to edit the whole thing together. He became that right arm to me. If there was one thing I was insecure about, it was my camera coverage, and I needed his expertise to see me through that. But the vision was mine and the show had a great look to it.

I felt very accomplished when we wrapped the pilot. It was a real growing experience and something I remain proud of. I returned to *The Nanny,* but I wasn't the same. I'd learned I could do other things, do them well, and do them independent of Peter.

Thanksgiving

Peter and I returned from hiatus refreshed and renewed. We were both unsure where our relationship was heading, but it was the sixth season of *The Nanny* and we entered it filled with hope and promise. Physically, though, I still wasn't myself. Other changes began to take place in addition to the staining and cramping, and it heightened my level of concern.

I seemed to be bruising really easily. On the show I was doing a lot of physical comedy, and for a time I blamed it on that, but after a while the bruises were so big and ugly they couldn't be considered normal. I remembered that movie *Marvin's Room*, where Diane Keaton went to the doctor for something unrelated and he noticed these massive black-and-blue marks all over her thighs. So he ran some blood tests and eventually diagnosed her with leukemia!

I just couldn't get that movie out of my head, and as if that weren't enough, I was also beginning to notice a change in my stool. And I ain't talking bar stools, either!

Now I was starting to connect the dots and wondered if all these changes weren't symptomatic of the same thing. So I decided to call my internist, Doctor #3. I'd already seen two gynecologists, who'd found nothing from my Pap test, pelvic exam, ultrasound, and mammogram. Based on the tests, it didn't seem like my problems were gynecological.

Meanwhile every attempt Peter and I made to connect outside the studio failed miserably. Everything we'd once had together seemed to have deteriorated, and all that was left was the show. We tried marriage counseling, but that didn't work. I don't think we were able to be completely honest with the counselor or each other, and after a few visits we abandoned that route. We tried to take a vacation together. I booked us in separate rooms, which was weird, but we were already living in separate homes, so what was weirder than that?

But I just wasn't strong enough as my own person to get back together with him. I was still feeling a profound regret that I'd wasted my youth being the good daughter and the good wife, but never truly knowing what *I* needed. What *I* wanted.

Then Peter invited me to Thanksgiving dinner at his new apartment. He included all the couples who were our dear friends. He catered it from a favorite restaurant, which we'd used for special occasions back in the ol' days when we were together. He even ordered my favorite wine. I arrived with candy, flowers, and music, attempting to be joyous and gay.

It couldn't have been easy for our friends who attended that night. To them, Peter and I were like an institution. Nobody but nobody would have ever imagined that of all the couples, we'd be the ones to split. Yet there we all were, trying to make the best of a very awkward situation. All the dinner guests were the same friends we worked with on the show, so there wasn't a lot of catching up to do, and the conversation bordered on the mundane.

"So how's everything?"

"Good, good. How 'bout you?"

"Fine, fine."

And that was the riveting stuff. Everyone was being so damned polite. Minding their p's and q's. It didn't seem like Thanksgiving at all. Growing up, it just wasn't Thanksgiving unless my mother got nervous and yelled, my sister got high-strung and slammed a few doors, and my dad overate to the point of indigestion and acute gastritis. Ah, the good ol' days.

I remember in my early married years with Peter, we'd sometimes spend the holiday gorging on Chinese food. Nothing like spareribs at Genghis Cohen when you're giving thanks. Another Thanksgiving we cooked for our friends but didn't want the leftovers because it was all so fattening, so we made plates of food for the homeless and eight of us piled into the old Buick and drove around L.A. looking for the needy. Believe it or not, it was a hard sell. No one wanted my home cooking!

But that was then and this Thanksgiving, unfortunately, had a whole different feel. For me it was a colossal push. It felt like a shoe that didn't fit. It was too much all at once: being in Peter's place, with all the friends I really hadn't been spending much social time with recently, and then simply Peter and I. We weren't who we used to be, and we had no clue who we were then, either. I felt so uncomfortable I couldn't wait for it to be over.

And I guess Peter sensed that things weren't right, because that night marked the turn of a dark corner in our relationship. When we returned to work, we fought the whole day. He said I didn't seem like the wife and best friend I'd been to him for over twenty years, but more like an acquaintance. The outburst left me confused, guilty, and sick to my stomach.

Neither of us ever recovered from that fight in his office. Elaine, our dear Elaine, who straddled that razor's edge of being manager and friend to both of us, was the glue that kept the ship afloat. "Keep working," she'd say to us. "Work is your salvation now." And we did keep working. She was there through it all, every step of the way, with all her glorious wisdom. Doing whatever it took, she kept us from self-destructing and from bringing it all down with us.

By the time I went to Doctor #3, my internist, I was whipped. Life seemed like one big grind and I didn't know if the rewards of being true to myself were worth the pain and heartache. Doctor #3 knew my life was in emotional turmoil and tried to ease my concerns over my physical ailments. He also downplayed my symptoms, chalking them up to a normal condition.

He checked my heart and my lungs. He looked in my ears, my eyes, and my nose. He felt my abdomen, even checked my reflexes. My pulse, normal . . . blood pressure, normal . . . everything, normal. In response to my short menstrual cycles, he concluded, "Normal is what's normal for you. If you've always had short cycles, then there's no reason to think there's a problem." As for the midmonth staining, he sided with Doctor #1's conclusion that I was at the threshold of being perimenopausal; he disapproved of the radical techniques of Doctor #2. Regarding my stool changing, he connected it to my diet, and told me I was "eating too much spinach."

So I decided to make an appointment with a hematologist, Doctor #4, to check out my blood. While I was there I thought he could check out my hormone levels, too. I was still afraid of the black-and-blue marks all over my legs and arms, though Doctor #3 didn't see it as a problem, since I'd always been a bit of a bruiser, and so was my mom. It was always a joke in our house each time my dad grabbed her arm too tight when he was showing affection. "Now I'm gonna be all black and blue! Why do ya have to be such a demonstrative lover?" she'd yell, socking him in the arm. Sort of the pot calling the kettle black, no?

None of my doctors, not even the hematologist, seemed particularly worried about my symptoms, so I tried to be light about the whole matter. I didn't want to worry my parents and I never even thought to call my sister, who's a nurse married to a doctor. Work continued to be such a huge distraction I didn't have much time to dwell on my fears anyway. I only kept pursuing more doctors because I wanted something that could be fixed. I didn't want to accept that I was perimenopausal and be stuck with that forever. It somehow didn't feel right.

We're Canceled

by the time January rolled around, all my coping mechanisms were fried. I simply couldn't deal with anything. People around me would wonder what kind of a mood I was in, or if I had PMS, if Peter and I were on speaking terms, or if we were fighting. I thought I was losing my mind, and I think so did everybody else.

My stress levels were through the roof. It was an out-of-control situation. Was I having a breakdown? Did I need to get off this treadmill I was on? What was it? As time went on the lower-abdominal cramping that had at first lasted only a few hours seemed to be stretching into a few days.

I felt scared, worried, misunderstood. I mean, even if the bruising and stool change weren't significant, the bleeding and cramping signaled something wasn't right, and at this point I wasn't even connecting them to my intense mood swings. The perverse contrast between my own life and my character on *The Nanny* was beyond ironic. There I was fearing the worst about my health situation, while Fran Fine was healthy as a horse. I was conflicted about having a baby, while she was pregnant with twins. She'd found the man of her dreams, while my marriage was coming apart at the seams. As topsy-turvy as it all was, I frankly relished the time I got to play Miss Fine, because her life was so much better than mine. She was funnier, happier, and less complicated. She became my refuge. It sounds sad because it *was* sad.

I remember one taping when I felt so vulnerable and under attack by Peter, who was directing from the control booth while watching my image on all four camera feeds. He scrutinized my costume and seemed overly critical about how I looked in it. In front of everyone. He asked me to change three separate times, and he still wasn't satisfied.

It might not have bothered me at all if I wasn't in such bad shape emotionally, but it sure bothered me then. I screamed to him through the camera, "You wouldn't treat another star this way!" I felt attacked, as though Peter were wielding his power as a weapon. Elaine sat in the booth with him as my image yelled at him on four separate screens. Later she'd tell me that he leaned over and whispered, "She's got to get on hormones." I definitely needed *something*. Maybe I was just being hypersensitive. Who knows?

Then my face started to break out, which really got me down. As an actress, I couldn't help feeling self-conscious going before the cameras with a huge headlight on my chin. The makeup department would make special provisions to try and conceal it, but I always knew it was there. Spackle might have been better. I remember saying I was glad this acne hadn't happened during my teens, because even as an adult with some perspective I was having trouble coping.

They weren't like regular pimples, either, but rather the kind that took forever to go away. And my breakouts began to occur with greater frequency until finally I was getting maybe two or three days of reprieve a month. The rest of the time I was frantically trying to arrest the situation. I'd go home and sit in front of my vanity and take off my makeup, exposing the acne I'd made best efforts to hide. All alone at night, I'd stare at my reflection in quiet desperation and weep. I swear, I was beginning to feel like Camille.

The strangest part of it all was how closely linked to my menstrual cycle my symptoms and emotional flare-ups were. Still, the blood tests that came back from the hematologist were all normal. No leukemia, diabetes, lupus. Hormone levels normal, platelets normal. Everything was fuckin' normal but me!

I was still in therapy and I remember describing what I thought was PMS and how hard it was when I felt like I was under its spell. One afternoon I was holding a writing session at my house when I noticed a favorite potted jade tree missing. Ramon had chopped it down and discarded it in the alley. I couldn't believe it. "Why did you do that? It was one of my favorite plants!" I ranted. Ramon had gotten the idea from someone that I didn't like it. He apologized and promised me it would grow back. So I walked over to the dining table where the writers were working and rejoined the session.

But I just couldn't let it go. I couldn't get over this travesty and so I put down my pen, picked myself up, and marched back out to him, where I really went ballistic. Ramon told me I was making him feel like this one mistake had erased everything good he'd ever done, and that's when I realized I'd gone too far. So I started backpedaling: "I didn't mean to do that. I'm very happy with the work you do. . . . I guess I'm just upset." I hugged him and retreated back to the writers.

The incident was so out of character for me that I discussed it with my therapist. I mean, I wasn't crazy or pathological; I *knew* I was acting strange. We concluded that the plant was me as a child. It was as if Ramon had hurt me and not the plant. *For this I'm paying $150 an hour?* But in fairness to my therapist, I did harbor a lot of sorrow for those times as a child when I was made to

sit by myself on the milk can outside our apartment door for mis-
behaving. Those times I felt scared, misunderstood, and unloved.
I guess when the plant was set aside in the alley my subconscious
reared its ugly head.

This satisfied me and seemed to explain why I'd overreacted,
but in retrospect I think it was much more than that. Perhaps on
some level I felt bad for the plant because I felt bad for me as a
child, but my reactions were definitely fueled by some kind of
chemical imbalance. No matter how deeply I dug into myself in
therapy to understand and unravel my past, I'd always end by saying the same thing. "This normally doesn't bother me, it's just
when I'm PMS-ing that I become so consumed by irrational anger
and insecurity."

And life wasn't getting any easier. A week later Peter and I were
called into the studio president's office. Something was up. We
walked together as we crossed the lot. For that moment we put
our personal differences aside. As we entered the inner chambers
of the top Columbia TriStar TV executives, they all seemed very
solemn. I noticed a framed *Nanny* poster hanging on the wall.
That was a good sign. I thought perhaps we were going to get the
usual ratings pep talk. I wondered if they knew Peter and I were
having problems. But the situation was much graver than that.

They began by saying that they'd gotten a call from the president of CBS. The network wasn't planning on renewing our option
for a seventh season. Our hearts sank. The show was the only
thread holding us together. It was our baby and now that, too, was
coming to an end.

After much persuasion by the studio and network, I agreed to
go public, announcing that it was *my* decision to end the show.
Better our audience think we were going out on top, by *my* choice,
than that we'd been canceled. There was some hope that if the
news came out midseason, it would somehow boost ratings and

prompt a miracle pickup. I hated the idea of pretending it was my decision because I didn't want everyone I worked with to think it was my fault they were losing their jobs. Nor did I want to be responsible for disappointing the millions of people who'd watched and supported the show all those years.

But pressure from the inside to do whatever it took to try to rescue our ill-fated show made me the fall guy. One of the hardest things I've ever done was to stand before my entire cast and crew, as well as Peter and the writer-producers, and make that speech telling them I was ending the show. "In my life I've always stayed too long at the fair, but not this time, not with *The Nanny*," I said, as my voice quivered.

Like real troupers, we were all inspired to wrap up the final episodes with style and panache. Some of our greatest shows emerged out of our despair, but for some reason unknown to me, the network that we helped keep afloat for so many years chose to abruptly pull us off the air. Brand-new episodes of *The Nanny* were shelved. Once the press release was out that I was the one quitting, the network quit us and I was left holding the bag. Elaine, as always, said it best: "I don't mind if you shove an umbrella up my ass, but when you open it, you've gone too far." That's why I love that woman!

Whatever was going down with the network, though, didn't affect the camaraderie that still existed on our stage. Within the world of *The Nanny* it was a time of expressions of love and gratitude. We who'd worked so hard and given our all for the show savored each and every moment we had left. There were many hugs and deep, tearful talks among us. We drank everything in so we wouldn't forget how glorious it all once was. We knew something very special, very precious, and extremely rare was about to end.

Friends

by the time we shot the final episode of the series my life had taken on a very different shape than at the time of the premiere episode six years earlier. The contrast was stunning; I often found it hard to believe myself. It was a bittersweet time to say the least. I didn't know what my life would be like without the husband and the show. As long as I had *The Nanny* to keep me busy day after day, week in and week out, I never felt true loneliness; nor did I have the opportunity to experience what being on my own was really like.

When the MTV pilot hadn't gotten picked up a few months earlier, I was disappointed, but a little relieved, too. Honestly, I didn't know how I was going to be able to service both shows at the same time anyway. But when we were told *The Nanny* wouldn't be returning for a seventh season, I called MTV and asked if we could retest the pilot if I edited it differently.

So during those final weeks of *The Nanny*, John and I tried to resurrect the pilot. I liked sitting in the editing room with him. Although I'd mostly been dating younger men, I really never got any vibe from him that he was attracted to me. However, it was during this time that we gradually became friends. I started planning group events with some friends from the show who all had fun partying together, John included. Everyone liked to dance and have a good time.

At the end of work, when the whistle blew, I needed to let loose. Often we'd pile into a limo so no one would drink and drive, then head out to a club or a restaurant for the night. I just loved being around this circle of friends. For me it recaptured a youth I felt I'd never truly experienced.

Am I too old to be acting this way? I wondered sometimes. I know I've always looked younger than I am, but some of these folks were twenty-five. We all got along so well and had so much in common, though, that age was never a factor. I guess it was right for me at the time.

I became closer to my cousin Erica, who worked on *The Nanny*. Our mothers are sisters, and it's nice to have family in L.A. Then there was this gal, Jill, who lived next door to me at the beach. When I met "good neighbor Jill," as I nicknamed her, I liked her right away. She became one of the first good friends I made outside of my marriage. She was single, fun, and high energy.

Erica, Jill, and I went to the Super Bowl in Miami a few years ago. We had so much fun people-watching and partying it up in South Beach. One night we found ourselves in a club with k.d. lang and Queen Latifah, cheering on Cher, who was lip-synching to her new single, "Believe." I was psyched to meet her, since I'd always felt a certain connection to her.

In therapy I'd often talk about Cher. She, too, had been in a famous marriage that began when she was very young. I didn't know her, but for some reason I identified with her. At first, when she and Sonny broke up, she seemed to have it all and be right in the center of things, but as the years went on, I thought she seemed lonely. I'm sure I was probably projecting my own fears of

loneliness onto her. Maybe she was ecstatic in her life and completely fulfilled. I hoped so, for both our sakes.

The next night we bumped into Ben Stiller and Chris Rock,
who were drinking and dancing with friends. Afterward, a bunch
of us piled into a limo and headed to Lenny Kravitz's house. That
was an amazing evening that carried into the wee hours. What a
simple girl from Queens was doing tripping the light fantastic
with the likes of Cameron Diaz and Edward Norton I'll never
know. (Sometimes I get starstruck, too, and have to pinch myself
to make sure I'm really there.) The evening's only downer came
when Lenny made us all take our shoes off before entering his
home. My untanned legs were all marked up from the boots I was
wearing, but thank God I'd shaved and had a pedicure!

Back in L.A. I remember we all went up to Ventura County for
a Phish concert. About eight of us loaded into a limo and headed
north. I love that band, and as it turned out, so did John. The two
of us were so enthusiastic about the whole event. That band draws
a big hippie crowd, so I was wearing my tie-dyed dress with peace
signs all over it. Go figure I would live long enough to see something go in and out of fashion and then come back in again!

On the car ride home, I observed John as he talked with endless enthusiasm to one of the other guys we were with. I'd never
known him to be so chatty. I guess he was beginning to relax a
bit more around me. Maybe I was becoming less of "the boss"
when we all hung out together, but he certainly seemed to be letting his shoulder-length hair down.

Usually there was something restrained about him. At work he
seemed like a different person: quiet, almost aloof, just doing his
job. He'd come to me with questions about the show, but he
didn't try to engage me in a personal way, even though the night
before we might have all been out dancing at the Martini Lounge.
He was definitely a conundrum. I did like working with him,

though. Everything he did he did well, and with the utmost professionalism. He had an even temper and was never moody.

Anyway, as much as I liked running with my new friends, my body kept reminding me that physically I couldn't keep up. I was experiencing a tenderness under my arms that I found worrisome. I still didn't know what was wrong with me. I'd seen four doctors already who'd told me I was fine.

When my armpit felt swollen and sore, I feared that whatever it was had gotten into my lymphatic system. So I made an appointment with Doctor #5, an oncologist and a breast specialist. When I entered his office, everyone who worked there was all smiles. I have to admit, it was a boost to my ego that they were so thrilled to meet me. Doctor #5 seemed particularly excited. As I lay on the table, he placed my right arm up over my head and began to feel my outer breast area. "You know, Fran, I have to tell you, I just love your show," he said, circling the nipple on my breast with his fingers. Look at this. Two of my favorite things, being fondled and flattered at the same time.

"Thanks, Doc," I giggled.

"I don't really see any problems here, Fran. But you know what I'm really surprised about?" Uh-oh.

"No, what?" I said, fearfully.

"That really *is* your voice."

"Who would make this up?" I responded.

It's strange having a physician who's a bit starstruck. But I guess it's difficult for most people to separate the real me from my TV persona. Once I went to the proctologist to treat a hemorrhoid. There I was with my ass in his face when he said, "Well, you've got quite the career going on there, don't you?" Now, what was I supposed to say to that—*Thanks, can I get off my knees now?*

Anyway, Doctor #5 read my mammogram and told me my

breasts were unusually dense for a woman my age: "You have the tits of an eighteen-year-old."

Well, if that didn't make my whole day. I didn't walk out, I floated. He'd told me what I wanted to hear: My body seemed young. It pacified me for the moment, but the truth is, I still left without a diagnosis. So I kept dancing as fast I could, burning the candle at both ends.

John

When we wrapped the show, Peter moved to New York for good. He and I pretty much knew it was over and that a divorce was imminent. I sold the dream house we'd so lovingly restored and dealt with the division of our estate. It was all very amicable and civilized. No children to complicate matters, just a clean cut in half with one lawyer to set up the dissolution of the marriage. Still, we couldn't speak to each other. We didn't know how to be, what to be, except what we always were: two completely codependent and neurotically entwined best friends. It was the end of an era.

Surprisingly, when the show ended John became more encouraging of our friendship. In fact, the little gang of friends who'd partied together during the last months of *The Nanny* continued to cling together long after its final curtain. I don't think any of us really wanted to disband right away, me least of all. The tighter I clung, the less I felt the deprivation.

One night I organized one of my group events at the House of Blues. It was an upper for all of us to once again eat, drink, and be merry. The band was great, and I found myself exchanging unexpected glances with John across the dinner table. Between us there were extra clinks of wineglasses and extra-close dances. I was picking up a vibe from John that I'd never experienced in all the years we worked together.

"Are you going to Vegas to see Phish?" he asked while we were dancing.

"Nah. I was thinking about it, if I could have hooked up with this guy I met in New York. But that's not going to happen, so I'm going to pass," I answered honestly. "Vegas isn't fun unless you can have a sexy time with someone. It's all so decadent, who needs to be alone?"

"Well, I'm going . . . maybe you should come anyway," he said, looking into my eyes.

Maybe I "should come anyway"? Was that a pass? I was totally caught off guard. John never seemed into me, so why had that one question seemed so loaded with possibilities? "Umm, uh, well, maybe. I don't know, should I?" What was I saying? I wished someone had stuffed a sock in my mouth.

By the car ride home it was clear he was indeed making a move, and I went for it. I've got to admit, up until this night I'd never seen it coming. He'd gotten that good at masking his feelings. Apparently, he'd had some relationships with coworkers in the past and they'd ended awkwardly. He vowed never to go down that path again.

I learned in therapy that we never know what's going on in anyone's mind. *He* wasn't thinking I was too old for him. That's what I was thinking he was thinking. The truth was, he liked me and always had. This twenty-six-year-old thought I was sexy, and believe me, I had no problem returning the compliment.

So that night I invited him in. Wow, I was so relieved that I liked the way he kissed, especially the way he held me when we kissed. He seemed to be having a great time, and was so open and uninhibited. When we undressed, I was glad I hadn't worn pants that left marks on my body. I've always liked being naked and felt surprisingly at ease around him. I think he found that refreshing and appealing. We had so much fun together. I never imagined he'd be such a confident lover. I don't know why I was so surprised—I mean, he was a great-looking young guy living on his own and making decent money. I'm sure he had a lot more experience with the opposite sex than I did! It's just that of all the good-looking guys working on the show, he was the only one who never flirted. He was like a mystery man, to me anyway.

In the morning I dropped him off at his place and said goodbye outside his apartment. He seemed uncomfortable with any public displays of affection and practically jumped out of the car, thanking me for the lift as if nothing had happened. All day I was thinking I should let him off the hook. I was the older one, in therapy and all; I should be able to communicate with him so things wouldn't get awkward or weird. I mean, what happened happened, but if the experience left him with regrets the next morning, we should be open and honest so we could remain friends.

Before I went to bed, I called him to see how he was. Basically, he was freaking out and grateful I'd called. He didn't want to speak with anyone about our encounter. He was very afraid of idle gossip, that he would now be thought of as Fran Drescher's boy toy. I could appreciate his concerns and respected him for being the kind of person he was, so I said, "Look, what happened last night was obviously something we'd both been curious about, and I'm glad we did it. It was fun. But we're not getting married and we never have to do it again, so no one needs to know."

He seemed very relieved by my tone, grateful I wasn't trying to get my hooks into him. Clearly, he felt way in over his head. All the

time I was hanging out with him, feeling like equals, he was looking at me as a huge star who'd also been his boss! I wasn't emotionally invested in him at all—I mean, I hardly knew him—so it
was easy to be grown-ups about the whole thing and resume being friends within our larger group of friends.

Well, I figured that was that, but that wasn't that because he
started calling me. He really didn't want things to end. He liked
what was beginning, but just got scared. The minute I cut him
loose, freed him of any and all obligation, he wanted me all the
more. Go figure.

So I guess you can say we very quietly started to see each
other. The more time we spent together, the more connected we
became. Like me, he always put other people's needs above his
own, and like me he had no clue that this was a way to avoid his
own problems and feelings. I think this common denominator became the magnet that held us together. We understood each other
because we both behaved the same way. And through this understanding, each of us was able to make huge progress in expressing
our wants and needs. It's not that his original concerns weren't legitimate or that his desire to be regarded on his own merit and not
for his involvement with me wasn't an issue. It was. By now, however, it was clear we could not stop seeing each other, so we simply kept our relationship a secret.

But my symptoms hadn't gone away. The regularity with
which I was having sex with John made the staining and cramping
a constant, though I really didn't feel comfortable sharing this
with him. I mean, I *loved* having sex with him. The way his long
hair tented around my face enclosed us in a dark, private world.
But every time we'd make love, I'd end up with a kind of mini period that was a real negative. So much for being the single swinger.

I didn't know where to turn, so believe it or not, I decided to go back to Doctor #1, the gynecologist I'd been seeing for years. I mean, I had wanted to try someone else and I did—I'd tried four someone elses, to be exact. And no one was offering me any miracles. So I was beginning to think that Doctor #1 wasn't so bad, and made myself an appointment.

The Progesterone Blues

September 1999

i was never one of those women who dreamed of having a baby. Not like my dear friend Rachel, who played Val on *The Nanny*. She always knew she wanted a baby and ended up giving birth to twins. My friend Donna had three daughters; my girlfriend Kat had three sons. It seemed like almost every woman I'd known wanted to have a baby and had one, including my sister. So why was I different? What was it about having a child that made me so scared? Not so much of rearing one, but of actually giving birth to one.

I used to wonder if I was just different from other women. I used to say, "I take care of Peter, it's enough." But really, that wasn't true. Actually, I think Peter would've made a good father. He always showed a lot of patience playing with other people's kids, whereas I didn't. But he wasn't that involved or loving toward Chester, our dog, which used to make me wonder. Still, none of that was relevant. In truth, the reason I never wanted children, which came out after having spent a lot of time in therapy, was that as a child I'd been told by my mother the story of how she'd almost hemorrhaged to death while giving birth to me. Because I was so fat.

When I brought this up with her only recently, she corrected, "I never said it was because you were fat, Fran. I said it was because you had a big head!" Whatever, be it fat or a big head, the drama that surrounded my delivery was a story I'd been told as far back as I can remember. It traumatized and repulsed me so much that it literally kept me from having a baby of my own. Maybe my mom thought I'd love her more if I'd known what she went through, but all it did was burden me with guilt and a fear that childbirth could be fatal.

Don't get me wrong—growing up, I felt loved and adored by my parents. I had a happy childhood. But I definitely possessed an overactive imagination, and found myself unable to slough off some of the vivid stories I was told.

Other little girls are told their births were the most beautiful experiences in their mothers' lives. So naturally, they grow up looking forward to the day of bliss when they'll become mothers, too. I, on the other hand, could only conjure up delivery-room chaos and blood spilling everywhere. The guilt I secretly harbored for having almost killed my mother was, without exaggeration, life altering.

Plus, she'd always gushed that I was the fattest, shortest baby in the hospital nursery. The fattest baby with the biggest head. "You were the most exquisite baby, but when Daddy put a comb under your nose you looked just like Stan Laurel," she'd say, laughing. That's it! Those are the details of my being brought into the world. Any wonder I never had kids? When I finally put all this together, a huge question mark in my life had been answered.

So there I sat, waiting for Doctor #1 to enter, thinking about John and how much he wanted someday to have children. Maybe for John I could overcome my fear. And babies were getting more appealing now that I no longer mixed them up with my own birth issues of fear and guilt. When Doctor #1 entered the examining room, I brought her up to date on the other four doctors I'd seen since my last visit with her. I needed to be up-front with her if we were going to reopen this investigation. She ordered some blood tests as well as an ultrasound. She did a Pap test and a pelvic exam. Same battery of tests, and again, everything normal.

"Well, you're too young for a D&C," she said matter-of-factly. And like an idiot, even though it was just a stupid test, I was flattered to be too young for it. In retrospect, I should have said right then, *Why, what would that show?* But I didn't. The only thing that ever showed up on a blood test was an elevated FSH (follicle-stimulating hormone) level, which is the messenger hormone in the brain that tells progesterone it's time to kick in. Since my FSH level was elevated, it seemed safe to assume that I was experiencing lower-than-normal progesterone. Doctor #1 once again held firm on the perimenopausal theory and prescribed progesterone pills as a hormone replacement therapy two weeks out of every cycle.

John knew I was experiencing some symptoms that had gone unexplained for some time and was hopeful that this prescription would solve the problem. He was very caring and understanding.

At this point, when my friends began to find out about us, he was just some guy who used to work on *The Nanny*—one sixteen years my junior and not even Jewish. Believe me, I vacillated over his significance in my life, too. I mean, I knew what a fine person he was. His instincts were always reliable. *Good upbringing,* I used to think. I appreciated his not wanting to exploit our relationship—many men would have felt differently. But *he* would have preferred it if no one knew ever, though that seemed too extreme for me. It was one thing to keep our unorthodox relationship private from the general public; it was another to hide it from our nearest and dearest.

Elaine was skeptical of it all, not for a moment thinking it could turn into something serious. "Honey, you worked very hard, you've been through a lot, enjoy him, he's a sweet boy." My friend Donna said, "You're not serious . . . are you?" And superficially I could see where those close to me might have thought this older woman–younger man relationship was a phase I was going through.

But I could see where others couldn't—beneath the surface. John wasn't the first younger man I'd dated since my separation, but he was by far the most special. And even though twenty-six sounded superyoung to Elaine, I remembered being twenty-six, and I felt younger at forty-two. Our friends always used to make fun of how middle-aged Peter and I seemed—already married and owning a condo.

Actually, our late twenties were the pits. A downward spiral of tragic events seemed to plague us. In about a three-year period, I underwent breast surgery, we became victims of a violent crime, both Peter's parents died of lung cancer, and his only remaining grandparent died, too, wiping out his entire immediate family. Those were hard years, and the last thing I felt like was a "girl." So it seemed condescending for Elaine to call John a "boy." She didn't even know him. I wondered if telling my friends about us was such a good idea after all. Meanwhile, I was falling for him and consumed over the age difference.

For me the gap in our ages took on heightened significance because I hated being forty-two. The number sounded so old. I didn't look forty-two, I didn't feel forty-two, and I didn't relate to being forty-two. This wasn't a healthy way to think. I know that now, but at the time I was regretful about not being freer in my youth and getting to know myself better. By denying my age I was trying to deny all the time I had wasted while being ruled by my need to be good.

The age issue wasn't a big deal for John, but I couldn't let it go. I knew we looked close in age now, but worried: What would we look like when he was thirty-five and I was fifty-one? Or forty-three and fifty-nine? Or sixty-two and seventy-eight? I drove myself nuts with the numbers.

Over and over, I talked about this with my therapist. Old when I was young, young when I was old, and fearful of losing both my looks and my youthfulness. I couldn't wrap my brain around what a freak I was.

I always thought about Ruth Gordon, the actress, who was so talented and youthful even when she was quite elderly. She always possessed charming energy and a little-girl quality. She was married for a long time to Garson Kanin, who was sixteen years her junior. On her deathbed he sat by her side and held her hand. He loved her to the end. Suddenly every show-biz older woman–younger man relationship fascinated me.

Ultimately, though, I decided that my worries about growing old, being abandoned and alone, really had nothing to do with John. I'd worried about this stuff all my life. In therapy, I connected these worries to empty threats my mother made to me as a child. Here we go again.

"I'm going to send you away to the home for bad children," she'd scream whenever my sister or I would get too out of control. And I don't know about my older sister, but I for one believed her! She never realized how frightened I was by what she was saying. Maybe on another child it wouldn't have had the same impact. But the mental images I created of this home for bad children became the core for all my fears of being alone, being unloved, being abandoned, and being dead. Once again, after I made those connections, I was able to let go of many of my lifelong fears. For the most part, I stopped worrying about getting old, about being alone, about dying. I stopped worrying about the age difference between John and me. I was just going to lighten up and get a sense of humor about it all, like when I first met John's buddy Nat. Shaking my hand, he said, "I'm John's oldest friend."

"And I'm John's oldest girlfriend," I responded happily.

I was able to color my hair in front of him and cover my gray without worrying about all that other crap. We'd joke about my "blond" growing out, but it was only a joke; we both knew it was gray. John would often tease me, "I'm going to send you away to the home for bad girlfriends if you aren't good." It was nice to finally be able to joke about it all.

Meanwhile, I wasn't the only one who needed to work on her problems. I'd begun to realize that John didn't like to travel and had a real fear of flying. Every time we made plans to go away, he'd become so stressed his immune system would weaken and he'd get sick. It was impossible to discuss plans with him because the very idea of it made him so nervous. The last thing I wanted was to make comparisons between John and Peter, but in this situation, it was difficult not to. I was running up against the same thing. Here was another man who didn't share my wanderlust.

"I know once I get there, I'll have a good time, but it's the getting there that's the problem," he'd say. For me, it was like being in a parallel universe, because those had been Peter's exact words, too. Verbatim! This was one area where I refused to indulge any man.

"If you give into this fear it will grow into a phobia," I'd always say. My desire was to always work through a fear rather than give in to it. I wished I could be with someone who actually looked forward to taking a great trip, but it just wasn't in the cards.

Then there were times when John would scold me for saying something he didn't think sounded good. Like when I said, "I'm going to the bathroom to take a dump." He suddenly became very parental and said, "Don't say 'dump.' It's a turnoff when you talk like a truck driver." I thought he was joking, but he wasn't. Now, I'd already gone through this sort of thing with Peter. There was no way, after everything I'd struggled through to get where I was,

I was going to end up with another man telling me what to do. Peter was a Scorpio, John was a Scorpio, and my father, the man who'd started it all, was a Scorpio, too. Are there no other signs of the Zodiac that I'm attracted to?

Oh my God, what's happening? I thought. Had I gone nowhere? Had I been standing still all this time? I really began to wonder. Was this part of John's Italian/Lebanese culture? I mean, where did he come off telling me what to do? On the upside, I liked the way I was responding in contrast to how I'd been with Peter. I didn't feel like I'd been bad, didn't worry John hated me or might leave. I never felt like I'd be sent away to the home for bad women who sounded like truck drivers. I simply felt he was more uptight than necessary, and that, for things to work out, it had to stop.

Of course, I needed to stop doing certain things, too. My inability to apologize has always been a problem. It was a problem when I was a kid, and in my marriage with Peter, as well as with coworkers and friends. During an argument I was also prone to name-calling, which John would take offense to. If I called him a baby, silly, or immature—to me, no big deal—he'd get really irritated. "Talk to me, communicate, don't call me names," he'd insist. He also made me aware of how many times I had, out of frustration, punched him in the arm. I guess I'd been doing that to boys since my girlhood and never thought much of it, but he didn't appreciate it at all. He was right. Name-calling and arm punching *are* immature and childish.

John and I fought a lot and cried a lot. At first we were always defensive about our own positions, but eventually we traced it back to pain in our childhoods, and that was when the tears came. Through our relationship we began to clean out the cobwebs of our past, put the pain aside, and see ourselves more clearly. I don't know how we were able to get through this time, but something kept us together. Whenever we figured out what was really behind a fight, it brought us so much closer. And with each discovery about ourselves, another brick was set in our foundation as we began to feel no one else knew us as well as we knew each other.

Meanwhile, nothing had changed symptomatically. My mood swings were still erratic, and Doctor #1's being so adamant that I was perimenopausal didn't help. The progesterone pills she told me to take two weeks out of every month might have helped a little, but not much. I was still staining, still cramping, still everything. When I called Doctor #1 and told her the progesterone didn't seem to be making much of a difference, she said, "Double the dose and see if that works." So I did.

It was right around this time that I was being honored in Amsterdam with the Silver Tulip Award. This is the Dutch version of the Emmy Awards, and *The Nanny* is a well-loved television series there. So John and I decided to make a vacation out of it for my birthday. We met my cousin Reid and his wife, Claudine, in Paris first, as well as my old friend Howie. He and I always daydreamed about the time when we would walk through the art museums of Paris together. And good neighbor Jill, who was working in Prague at the time, planned to fly in for the weekend. After about a week in Paris, our plan was to take a train up to Amsterdam, where we'd do the awards show and enjoy the city before returning to the States.

Unfortunately, I was having a horrible reaction to the double dose of progesterone—something I didn't realize until it was almost too late. If I'd had mood swings before, now I was completely jumping out of my skin. I really felt insane, had no coping mechanisms. My face broke out worse than ever. I felt like I was capable of murdering someone or killing myself.

Everything upset me on that trip. There were brief episodes when I felt free-spirited, but probably only after a few glasses of wine. The rest of the time I was pulling my hair out of my head. Nothing was going right for good neighbor Jill, either. She hated her hotel, the cabbie took her to the wrong place, her shoes were killing her, and I was intolerant of her problems. John and I fought, and Howie, having worked with me for so long on *The Nanny,* knew to keep his distance until the coast was clear. Claudine and Reid had each other and, thankfully, were very independent. I remember John yelling at me, "You're acting crazy. I can't be with someone who acts so crazy!" My behavior was costing me my relationship with him, as well as some friendships I very much valued.

The train ride to Amsterdam was interminable. I thought I'd lose my mind. What people must have thought of me, I don't know. One morning John and I woke up feeling intensely unhappy. During room service in our beautiful suite overlooking a quiet, leafy, tree-lined canal in Amsterdam, I realized something that hadn't occurred to either of us before. *"It must be the pills!"* I remember saying. "There's something wrong with me, I'm not acting normal. This is not me and I think it's these stupid pills I'm on." I guess this rang true for John, too. Suddenly a whole new light was cast on the situation and his tone changed from angry to calm.

"Well, what are you going to do? You have to take the pills," he said.

"No I don't!" I responded with conviction. "Not if they're ruining my life I don't. This can't be what I need. It just can't be. . . ." Upon my return from Europe I called Doctor #1 and described my extreme reaction to the pills.

Without skipping a beat she said, "Well, why don't you try

taking half the dosage and see how you feel?" I'd started by taking one pill in the first place, before doubling it to two in the second place! Jeez, what was she thinking? Right then and there I decided that was it for Doctor #1. *Au revoir.* I never, ever wanted to see her again.

The Pill

i should have known 2000 was gonna suck when on New Year's Eve, in front of my house, a driver smashed into poor Howie's parked car and totaled it. Fire trucks, policemen, and neighbors were congregated out there trying to sort through the damage and mess. For security's sake, I sat inside watching the action on my monitor as my party guests milled around outside taking photos and trying to calm down Howie. He eventually went home in a taxi around ten-thirty P.M. with a doggie bag of food and about ten milligrams of Valium. Happy New Year! From that point on the rest of the year only got worse.

I continued to suffer from all the usual symptoms, and just to add to the list, I now began to experience a nagging leg pain. It was mostly in my left leg, and occurred mostly at night. It had gotten so bad I hated going to bed. Every night the same thing. I couldn't sleep without taking some kind of painkiller or sleeping pill. I tried lying with pillows under my legs, wearing socks, rubbing BenGay, using a heating pad, even filling hot-water bottles. Sexy, huh? But nothing, and I mean nothing, worked. I felt like I was falling apart and wondered if all this stuff was the nagging aches and pains of impending old age. Did I just need to learn to live with it? I was at my wit's end, in desperate need of help. So I made an appointment with a vascular specialist, Doctor #6. I mean, the leg thing was the worst symptom of all. I was like a trapped wild animal. If I didn't get help soon, I was gonna chew my leg off!

I remember Elaine had spent a year complaining about leg pain before being diagnosed with a blocked artery by a vascular doctor. Up until that point she'd been told she needed back surgery for a compressed disc. Her fear of surgery kept her searching for another diagnosis, though, and she eventually found her way to *Mind Over Back Pain* by Dr. John E. Sarno. This doctor's approach sounded nonsurgical to Elaine, so she pursued it.

An associate of Sarno's listened to her symptoms and asked her what no other medical doctor had thought to ask: "Have you had a Doppler flow test?" Wouldn't you know it? That one little test, easily and painlessly performed in a doctor's office, told the whole story of her leg pain. The cause was a blocked artery in her leg, which required bypass surgery. At least she was getting operated on for the right thing, and it did fix her. The lesson here is that if you're experiencing pain, numbness, weakness, or weird sensations in any of your limbs, or if you seem sluggish in your head, a bit out of it, just not as sharp as normal, you may have a blocked artery. I don't know why doctors don't offer this test regularly.

So there I was, describing all my symptoms again to the vascular specialist, Doctor #6, wanting this Doppler flow test, too. He used a wand that looked like an ultrasound and scanned my arterial system for any blockages. But once again the test showed nothing. "You probably have night cramps," he blurted out.

"What are those?" I questioned.

"No one knows why we get them, but they're very common. I've been told tonic water helps," he said, while cleaning up his tools.

"Tonic water?" I asked, incredulous.

"Yup. Do you like gin and tonics?" he inquired.

"I never had one," I answered.

"Well, try having one before you go to bed, lemme know if it helps," he said, exiting. Now, I gotta admit, a gin and tonic is a tasty thing at around 11 P.M. with the fireplace goin' and the TV on . . . it didn't do much for the leg pain, though.

It was all so crazy. One doctor told me I had the tits of an eighteen-year-old, one doctor said I was eating too much spinach, and this guy thought I should drink gin and tonics at bedtime. So there I was with perky breasts, in need of roughage, going to bed sloshed, all in some futile attempt to cure myself.

That's when I called the neurologist, Doctor #7, thinking maybe it was neurological. He requested an MRI (magnetic resonance imaging) of the hip and leg area. An MRI is not an X ray, but a machine that uses magnets to create its images. This was my first one and I was a bit nervous. Would I get claustrophobic?

I'd heard from many people that the cylinder you're slid into is very small. I was told they have open models and closed models. The open models aren't as thorough as the closed models, and the closed models, while more thorough, are very confined. Well, it was all true and of course, my luck, for some reason unknown to me, I had to use the closed model.

I went with John. The MRI, by the way, isn't a quick test. It's a very exact science and in my case ended up taking close to an hour. They gave me earplugs "because the device is a bit noisy." Well, that's the understatement of the century, since it's a cacophony of machine-gun-sounding bells, buzzers, and bangs. They offered me mirrored eyeglasses that would enable me to see John while in the cylinder. My dad said he'd just closed his eyes when he had to get an MRI but, I must admit, I was beginning to feel a bit anxious just looking at the contraption. And that was on five milligrams of Valium.

So I put on the mirrored glasses and John sat on a chair behind my head, but in the same room. Then, through the reflection in the special glasses, I was actually able to see John behind me. There he was, his sweet face and calming presence, smiling and comforting me the entire time. I'm so glad I was given those glasses! They made all the difference.

The MRI results came back completely clean. So Doctor #7 gave me Neurontin to take at night. It helped alleviate the pain, but not my problem. R.L.S. (restless leg syndrome) was the closest thing to a diagnosis I ever got. The pills did help, but no connection was made between my leg pain and my other symptoms.

Over lunch the next day with my friend Dorothy, I confided in her about my health problems. She'd directed many episodes of *The Nanny,* but we'd been friends for years before that, and I knew I could trust her. She suggested I see *her* gynecologist, an expert on women's midlife health issues and hormone replacement. She said this woman had saved her; that she now felt full of vim and vigor. I had to admit, she looked great. Apparently, this doctor had written many books and made countless television appearances on the subject of women over forty. With renewed optimism I made an appointment with Doctor #8.

In the meantime, John had come up with a clever concept for MTV. I liked it, so I called my contact over there to pitch it. When I gave the guy our one-liner, he said they were already in development on a similar idea. It's unbelievable how tough it is to come up with something original. But the executive said we should come in and brainstorm *other* ideas. John thought that was it for his ideas and didn't want to take the meeting.

"Are you crazy?" I asked. "When the head of a network says, 'Come in and brainstorm,' you go!" Even as I said it I was questioning my sanity over even considering working on a project with John after everything I'd been through with Peter. Separation of church and state had been my intention for all future relationships. Whoops.

Well, we spent a long, hard day trying to concoct ideas, with few results. We were both hungry and tired, so I ordered in some Chinese. I've loved Chinese food ever since I was a kid. Just as I shoveled in a forkful of roast pork lo mein, John blurted out an idea. A show about a local telethon—everything that goes on both behind the camera and in front. The minute he said it, I knew that was it. Oh, I really enjoyed my egg foo yong after that.

MTV loved the idea and ordered a script. That was the beginning of John's and my writing collaboration. I never learn. I did love creating a world with John, but creation is very hard, and we fought over everything. Sometimes I wanted to kick myself for getting involved with it. But I guess I'm just a hopeless optimist or a complete idiot. I've not yet decided which.

So, okay, we got along, we communicated, we were attracted to each other, but he someday wanted to have children and I was perimenopausal. *Oy.* I began to worry that my eggs were getting old and if the day came that we ever did want to have a baby, it would be too late. Between the staining, the cramping, and the leg pain I felt like I had maybe an hour of fertility left. So even though we'd only been together a year, and hardly ready to talk about this, I got it in my head that we should fertilize some eggs and freeze them. Currently, the technology to successfully freeze an unfertilized egg is in the earliest, experimental stage. I figured that when and if we felt ready to start a family, we'd already have a few embryos ready to go, no matter what the current status of my ovaries may be. This process is a common technique used among couples with conception problems, or couples hedging against the march of time, as in my case. I loved the idea!

But John hated it. He wasn't ready. Honestly, *we* weren't ready, and he turned me down flat. I mean, I didn't know if I wanted kids, but I knew I wanted to keep all my options open. There I was, forty-two years old, my eggs withering away with each menstrual cycle, and my last-ditch attempt at reproduction was being squelched by my twenty-six-year-old boyfriend. I felt trapped by circumstances and anxious about the impending menopause and all its ramifications. Here's where I think our age difference became a major problem. John and I weren't on the same page—hell, we weren't even in the same book!—and I felt hurt and alone.

One word led to another and I, who by now was feeling not only rejected but also old and misunderstood, said, "Maybe we should see other people." I mean, he wasn't budging and I wasn't gettin' any younger. I just couldn't see what possible reason would justify not taking the steps now that would prepare for our possible future later.

The moment I said it, we both started to cry. Why was this happening? It wasn't what either of us wanted, but somehow this baby thing had become a major bone of contention. "Maybe we shouldn't do this," I said, and we both laughed through our tears. Then he left for work and I closed the door behind him.

I spoke to many friends that day. One person thought we were such a great couple that she was not only surprised, but disappointed that our relationship had taken this unexpected turn. And the truth was, I had never even wanted children, so it was pretty ironic that that's what we might be breaking up over. But there we were. I just hated the whole situation, yet I didn't want to live with regrets, either.

I spent the whole day thinking about and digesting what had gone down that morning. John came back to my house after work. We hugged in the entry hall and although we both knew this issue wouldn't go away, neither of us really wanted to break up over it. So for the moment, we agreed to disagree and made up.

It was really all academic anyway. I mean, I was getting all wound up about fertility and frozen embryos because the doctors kept telling me I was perimenopausal. But that was a misdiagnosis. Fertility was the least of my problems.

I just wanted to feel good again. I wanted to have sex without cramps. I wanted my complexion to be nice again. I wanted to feel more even emotionally. I had to get rid of my leg pain. That, more than anything, was really getting me down. I honestly felt like I was at the end of my rope. The longer I went without a diagnosis, the worse I felt and the more I feared that when they figured out what it was, it wouldn't be caught in time.

Perhaps Dorothy's gynecologist, Doctor #8, would help me once and for all. As the elevator doors opened, I entered her posh and spacious waiting room. Doctor #8, the guru of middle-aged women, the maven of hormone replacement therapy, had copies of her books strewn on tables throughout the waiting area. I perused their pages while waiting for my name to be called. Now, I know a lot of women, but I don't know a single one who actually likes going to the gynecologist. I mean, what's to like? It's the ultimate invasion of privacy. Stripping down, spreading your legs. Talk about feeling vulnerable. I was so sick of it all.

As I sat in my examining gown on the table awaiting Doctor #8, I found myself thinking about Gilda Radner. During her struggles with cancer, she wrote a book titled *It's Always Something*. Peter read it first; we both loved her from *Saturday Night Live*. In her book she urged women to pursue as many doctors as it takes until you get a diagnosis, if you believe there's something wrong. Poor Gilda, she was put through the wringer; by the time she finally got diagnosed with cancer, it was too late. She wrote about her leg pains, encouraging women to consider them a symptom of gynecological cancer, even though the medical community still doesn't recognize them as such.

I remember seeing photos in the book of her with her little dog.

A Yorkie. She never went anywhere without that dog. Just like me and Chester. My friend Danny Aykroyd used to say she was a nice person, a good person. Years after she died, Peter and I spotted Gene Wilder at the Rancho Valencia Resort. There he stood at the front desk with that same little Yorkie, her dog. It broke my heart to see them together, without her. It was an image I'll never forget.

When Doctor #8 entered the room I ran down the litany of my symptoms, and included Gilda's story, leg pain and all. I told her I'd been staining for two years. As for Gilda, Doctor #8 said she wasn't sure what exactly Gilda had, but that it had been well over a decade ago and that a lot had changed in women's medicine since. The leg pain she dismissed as unrelated. It was the imminent last tick of my biological clock that piqued her interest as she barreled into a series of questions.

"Are you involved with anyone?" she asked.

"Yes, I am," I answered.

"Do you plan to have children?" That's a touchy subject, next question.

"Have you considered a fertility doctor?" Boy, was she pressing all my buttons.

Honey, I'm bleeding between periods, can we focus on the issue at hand? I wanted to say, but sheepishly answered, "John is quite a few years younger than I am, and not ready, plus my divorce isn't even final yet, so we decided to wait a little longer." She seemed disappointed in that answer as she reexamined my chart. I just knew she was focusing on my age as she grunted, "Hmm . . ."

We did an ultrasound in her office as well. She noticed a slight thickening of the uterine wall, which she said birth control pills would take care of, but saw no tumor of any kind. "Your ovaries look fine, your uterus looks fine," she said, showing me the monitor, but all I could make out was swirls of gray and patches of dark gray. I didn't know what she was seeing.

She told me my symptoms did *not* indicate cancer, but rather a perimenopausal hormone imbalance. "As for the progesterone Doctor #1 put you on, that wouldn't have been my choice," she said. "Birth control pills are the way to go!" she exclaimed with great confidence. I never realized that if you take the pill for even six months it can reduce your risk of ovarian cancer by as much as 50 percent. I told her that when I was a teenager I'd tried the pill to help relieve severe menstrual cramping, and that I hadn't reacted well to it at all. But Doctor #8 shook her head and said condescendingly, "The birth control pill has improved greatly since the 'seventies, Fran." *Well, aren't I just an old battle-ax from the Dark Ages.* She assured me I wouldn't have any noticeable reaction this time around, except possibly some bloating and slightly enlarged breasts. Okay, let's just say the enlarged breasts sounded good and leave it at that.

I never really liked the idea of a birth control pill. It seemed unnatural to me. All my sexual life I used condoms, and not the ones with the spermicide, either. I was used to them. I really never knew any different, and aside from the occasional wrapper stuck to my ass, I liked them. It seemed easy, safe, and clean. I'd keep some in my purse at all times so I could always be spontaneous. I even kept a few in the shower. Because ya never know. . . . The concept of taking the pill was new to me, but I decided to give it a whirl. She seemed so sure and confident in her diagnosis, I wanted to remain open. Maybe she knew what she was doing.

We also discussed a fertility doctor whom she thought was very good, and she urged me to speak with John about seeing him. I thought that the doctor's also being Lebanese couldn't hurt. When I saw John that evening we both had something to say on the subject. He'd given it a great deal of thought and decided he wanted to go ahead with the frozen embryo idea, but there'd have to be one made with someone else's sperm as well. In the event we broke up, and I still wanted a child, I wouldn't use *our* embryo, but instead use the embryo not related to John. He said he couldn't bear the thought of a child of his growing up in this world without him in its life. I respected that, and I appreciated that he continued to think about it. He'd come up with a solution that would satisfy my needs and accommodate his as well. What a doll.

Somehow I had renewed confidence in the situation. Doctor #8 was very affirmative and sure nothing was seriously wrong with me. John was definitely into the Lebanese fertility doctor as the way to go and showed enthusiasm toward the switch from condoms to birth control pills. In that brief moment in time there was a feeling of suspended animation and calm. But it was all smoke and mirrors, because the shit was about to hit the fan. *Big-time.*

The Botero and the D&C

now that the show was over, I decided this was the time to reorganize and finish decorating my house, do all the things I never had time for during the series. My apartment had become too small and lacked privacy, so after a year I'd bought a loftlike modern house that was much more suited to my needs. There I was, living in my new, beautiful beach house and still putting my silverware in the drawer Angelica had placed it in the day I moved in. At the time I was too busy with the show to even unpack, let alone put things where I thought they should go. So getting my house in order seemed like an appropriate thing to do. My therapist had always said cleaning and organizing is a productive extension of your need to do the same mentally. So I started with the drawers and closets. I put things where I preferred them to be, and carried the process through to the art and furnishings.

I love art. I remember my mom once bought me a book on van Gogh that I cherished. As a kid I always loved to draw and sketch. As an adult I became more knowledgeable about art appreciation and collecting through my friendship with Elaine and Allan. It enriches me to no end. I love looking at auction catalogs, going to art museums, and learning to recognize different artists from many different genres. I mean, where I came from fine art was a paint-on-velvet picture of a man in a sombrero. But now it's a passion of mine. When John and I first became friends, art was not a common denominator—not until he spent an afternoon with Howie and me walking through the Louvre in Paris. Our enthusiastic discussions about the pieces sparked John's interest, and he soon developed his own appetite for fine art. John and I began to enjoy both a sexually and intellectually stimulating relationship, I'm happy to say. It was becoming the full flavor of the bean, and who doesn't like flavorful beans?

I had my eye on a few pieces of art from the upcoming Billy Wilder collection auction at Christie's and decided to go to the viewing. I fell in love with a Botero sculpture. A gorgeous rotund female nude, lying on her side, bathed in bronze. She was magnificent. I just knew that if I owned her, I'd make her the centerpiece of my living room. Howie helped me research what similar pieces had gone for at auction in the past so I could make an informed decision about whether to bid on her, and how high to go before I'd be going overboard.

Meanwhile the birth control pill wasn't giving me the pimples or irritability I'd felt from the progesterone, but it was suddenly making me bleed 24/7. What the hell kind of a cure was this? While the progesterone from Doctor #1 seemed to reduce the midmonth staining, the birth control pill from Doctor #8 seemed to increase it. After about five days I called Doctor #8, who was quickly losing her appeal. She was out of town doing television appearances and wouldn't return to L.A. for a few days. *Nu?* She's got a better career than me. When she finally called me back, I told her the pill seemed to be worsening my symptoms. The bleeding was quite heavy and nonstop, and my leg cramps were bothering me more than ever. Annoyed and disappointed, I said, "This *can't* be the right treatment for me!"

She told me to stop the pill. It was Tuesday, and I'd been taking it for only a week. She said she could see me on Thursday, first thing in the morning, and just as a precautionary measure, she'd do a D&C to scrape some tissue from the uterus for biopsy, but I probably was just taking too low a dose of birth control pills. Her advice didn't strike me as logical. How could it help to take a higher dose of a substance that was already *worsening* my symptoms?

But that was what she said, so I stopped the pill in anticipation of the procedure on Thursday morning. On Wednesday night the Billy Wilder collection was going on the auction block in Beverly Hills, and John and I got dressed in business attire so we'd look serious and classy for our first live art auction. It was all prearranged: my credit with the auction house, my copy of the catalogue . . . I even got a paddle with a number! We were meeting my agent and his wife, who are major art collectors, followed by a dinner at Mr. Chow. I wore something black and slimming, since I thought my stomach was more distended than usual.

It was very exciting. As each lot number came up on the auction block, the bidding was displayed in seven different currencies up on the wall. An attractive Indian woman stood behind the podium with a gavel and about half a dozen Christie's reps lined the wall, all holding telephone receivers ready to relay phone bids from art enthusiasts throughout the world.

John and I sat in the back row. When the Botero sculpture bidding began, about ten people raised their paddles, myself included. Now, I'd been told by friends who are serious collectors that it's always best ahead of time to put a limit on how high you'll go. This is to prevent getting swept up in the excitement and overpaying. Famous last words.

So I set my limit, the final figure beyond which I wouldn't go higher. Within no time at all every paddle in the place was down except for mine and a Christie's caller on the phone. The caller made the last bid, which was of course above my preset limit. The auctioneer looked at me to go higher. "What should I do? She's lookin' at me."

"Don't do it," John whispered.

"The lady in the back, does the lady in the back want to make a bid?" *Me?* I was the lady in the back? People were turning around to see the response from the lady in the back. I pressed my paddle into my lap and nervously shook my head no. She got my drift and searched the room again. "Anyone else, anyone at all?"

I'd never realized how forceful these auctioneers can be. Positively pushy. I mean, they look in your face and *will* you to raise that paddle. But John was muttering under his breath, "It's too expensive, it's too high." With no new paddles entering the bidding, she had to turn to her only remaining bidder on the phone. "All right then, going once, going twice . . ."

Suddenly a little voice inside me spoke to me as clear as a bell. *Don't let her go to some stranger's house, she belongs with you.* Now, I don't know who that big mouth was buzzin' in my head, but with that my paddle shot up, and in the true tradition of live auctions, everyone in the room gasped and turned to see the celebrity in the back row take it home! The auctioneer then turned back to the phone rep, hoping she still had a horse race, but the phone rep simply shook her head, and the auctioneer quit while she was ahead. She pounded her gavel on the podium and shouted, "Sold to the lady in the back!"

I didn't know whether to celebrate or vomit, but we already had reservations at Mr. Chow so it only made sense to celebrate now, vomit later! On our way out we ran into a big television producer I'd worked with in the past. My agent had told me this guy was a serious art collector, and since he'd bought the other Botero in the collection for his wife I felt more confident about my purchase. I figured if it was good enough for him, it was good enough for me.

Mr. Chow is always a crowded Beverly Hills scene, and we were kept waiting for a while at the front. This only gave me time to slip back into worrying about my impulsive expenditure. But as fate would have it, the table we were waiting for was occupied by Billy Wilder himself! Well, if seeing the producer had been a positive sign, seeing Billy Wilder really got my appetite going.

As the great director exited the restaurant in a wheelchair pushed by a cheerful Asian man, I leaned down to Mr. Wilder and said, "I bought your Botero sculpture!" Well, the man pushing his wheelchair seemed happy, but I got absolutely no response from Billy, and wondered if perhaps he was a bit hard of hearing. It didn't matter; to me the stars seemed aligned and good signs were everywhere. So bring on the spareribs.

All night I had such indigestion from my anxiety that I barely slept. Why was I spending so much money on an inanimate object when I didn't even know what was wrong with me? I felt like I'd made a terrible mistake, like I'd been frivolous and indulgent. It has always been so difficult for me to splurge on things for myself. Except, of course, on food, for which I'll spend any amount. I was so anxious and regretful, I cannot even tell you. This, in the auction biz, is commonly known as "buyer's remorse." But alas, when you buy at auction, there are no exchanges, no refunds, no nothin' but the bill. That chubby bronze naked lady was mine, like it or not!

John thought I was just nervous about the D&C. I wasn't sure if it was that or the sculpture, but nevertheless I needed to get my ass out of bed and rush to get ready before I missed my appointment. In the car I noticed I was indeed running late and immediately called Doctor #8's office to let them know. They put my mind at ease and told me not to worry; they'd be awaiting my arrival whenever I got there.

Then I called Howie, whom I was supposed to meet for breakfast after my appointment. The mounting traffic made it doubtful
I'd fit it all in. I literally broke down in tears to the poor guy, who
was not only hungry but had his own problems, since he was
scheduled for knee surgery the next day. I'm not sure whether it
was the sculpture, being late, or not knowing what was wrong
with me, but suddenly I was overwhelmed with fear and sorrow.
Fortunately, Howie was able to calm me down on the phone as I
pulled into the medical building's garage.

Upon entering Doctor #8's office, I found the waiting room
empty and tranquil. The nurse greeted me with warmth and led
me into the examining room. Once again I undressed and put on
the cover-up. Doctor #8 wanted to shoot me with Novocain before doing the D&C. In retrospect I wouldn't have taken this extra
step. The shots themselves were painful and then I had to hang
around in the examining room for at least ten minutes before they
started to work. In that time I could have had the procedure done
and been finished already instead of just beginning. Plus, the Novocain failed to dull my pain.

While I was waiting for the Novocain to kick in, Doctor #8
launched back into her favorite topic. "Have you set an appointment for you and John to meet with the fertility doctor?" *Oy, what's
with all these doctors? Can't she give it a rest? I'm bleedin' 24/7 here.*

"Not yet, I'm sort of concerned about the D&C, to tell you the
truth," I replied. But she was convinced this procedure was
merely a precaution and still held firm that hormone replacement
was the answer. I called Howie on my cell and told him they hadn't
even started yet and that I thought breakfast was a bust. There I
was, full of Novocain up my *yitz,* chatting on my cell phone about
breakfast plans. Talk about surreal.

The D&C was definitely painful, but literally took no more
than two minutes. It felt like a Pap test, only worse. Given the brief

amount of discomfort involved, I believe it's something that should be offered right away to any woman of any age who's experiencing midmonth staining, cramping after sex, or unusual weight gain. Two minutes of discomfort right in your doctor's examining room should be the worst of your problems. For me it was just the beginning. It would take three days before I'd receive the results. So I dressed, got back in the car, and drove directly to a furniture store to buy a new coffee table for my Botero.

"It's Cancer"

When the phone rang I was in the bathroom. Since becoming single I always like to have a handset wherever I am in the house, in the event of an emergency. As long as the phone is within arm's reach, I'm never really alone. When I heard it was Doctor #8 I went into my bedroom to grab a pen and paper. I'd learned from experience: When speaking with a doctor about anything that concerns you, get in the habit of taking notes.

That's when it happened. In that moment. Reality with a capital R came and bit me on the ass. On the phone, sitting on the edge of the bed, in my workout clothes, clutching a tiny pad, I wrote down that I had cancer as tears rolled down my cheeks.

How could this be happening? How could this be true? No one else said I had cancer, and I'd had blood tests. Isn't cancer supposed to be indicated by your blood count? I'd had many ultrasounds of my uterus—why didn't the cancer show up there? Why, why, why?

I hung up the phone in a complete state of shock. Was I going to die? Was I now to become another medical statistic? How could this have been going on for so long undiagnosed? Scribbled on my pad was an appointment on Friday to meet with a gynecologic oncologist. *Friday?* But this was Monday! How could I, why should I have to wait four days before taking the next step? You know what my answer was? "Because that's when she sees new patients." Who cares about some new-patient policy when I have cancer, for God's sake?

But the world doesn't change itself because you have cancer. The only world that changes is yours! I opened my bedroom door slightly and could see Ramon and Angelica putting fresh flowers in vases.

"Ramon, is Leesa here?" I asked, trying to maintain control.

"Yes, Fran, she's upstairs waiting for you," he said, walking over.

"Can you tell her to come down please?" I asked. He then instructed Angelica in Spanish, *"Dile a Leesa que venga para abajo,"* and she dropped what she was doing and hurried upstairs.

"Thank you, Ramon," I said, as I began to close my door.

"Fran, I'm thinking about getting a hot dog stand, what you think about that?" He always comes up with these "Ralph Kramden" ideas and bounces them off me.

"I think all the good street corners are taken, Ramon," I answered, trying to remain calm.

As I retreated into my room, I could hear him mumble, "Ooh, I never thought of that. . . ."

When Leesa entered my room she said, "What's the matter, honey, is everything okay?"

Crying, I said, "The doctor just called and said I have cancer." I threw my arms around her and wept on her shoulder. She sat with me on the bed as I paged John with the 911 code. This, we decided, would only be used for true emergencies—like if Chester, my geriatric dog, died, or something of that significance. Well, I figured it didn't get more significant than this, and dialed it in.

Leesa and I had become friends over the course of our workouts together. I was new to the neighborhood, but she seemed to know where to go for everything—the best seafood, the best hikes, even where to get your car washed. I liked her from the start. She was blond and pretty, very chatty, and a devoted wife and mother.

While waiting for his return call, Leesa, who was in a difficult situation at best, thought she'd lighten up the moment by telling me a story about her dog and a sick bird she'd rescued. But what to her seemed like a light and humorous tale took for me a weirdly macabre turn when the bird got trapped in the bathroom with a claustrophobic dog. In its panic the dog got caught up in the towel the bird was resting in and inadvertently killed it.

"*Oy*, that's an awful story," I exclaimed. "I feel so bad for the bird," which I immediately identified with. And this was supposed to be funny?

Poor Leesa, all she could say was, "I guess it *is* kinda horrible. I don't know why it seemed funny at the time. . . ."

When the phone rang, thank God it was John. First words out of his mouth were, "Sweetie, what's the matter?"

"The doctor called and said I have cancer."

"Oh my God, I'm coming right now. I'll be there in forty-five minutes." What he said was so perfect, it still chokes me up when I think of it. "Is anybody there?" he went on to ask. "I don't think you should be alone." I told him I was with Leesa, and that Ramon and Angelica were there, too. "Okay, I'm leaving right now, I love you," and he hung up. He later told me he'd run like a madman into his boss's office, said his girlfriend had just found out she had cancer, and he had to leave at once.

It's a blessing when the person you love shows the kind of instincts you'd hoped they'd have when push comes to shove. Illness is the great equalizer. It doesn't matter who you are, rich or poor, young or old, fat or thin, *sick is sick*. And if you're blessed, those around you will rise to the occasion in your hour of need.

The next call I made was to my parents. Now, who wants to call their parents and tell them their child has cancer? What a monumentally difficult task it was, for me anyway. You see, the nature of my relationship with my mother and father had been one where I'd always tried to be the worry-free child, in contrast to my sister, whom they worried about constantly. My mom gets scared easily by many, many things and worries about everything, but especially her loved ones. For me, being the cause of any pain for them went completely against the grain. I always felt like I had to be strong for them.

Years ago, after the "break-in" (our euphemism for the rape), I'd found it so impossibly hard to tell them that my sister was the one who had to make the call. I was so worried about them, I couldn't allow myself to turn to my own parents after being raped at gunpoint. It was always so twisted in my mind. I thought I knew what was best, but I never even gave them a chance to show strength.

When my sister was about eight, she had a seizure on the playground one afternoon. At the hospital I witnessed my mother completely lose it, and it frightened me. My mother was so sad, so upset, so hysterical. I never wanted to be the cause of that. I developed the bad habit of denying my own needs.

Well, this time was going to be different. I hadn't been in therapy for three years not to be able to put myself first. I'd learned how to be human, to be able to take as well as give, to sometimes be needy and feel justified in my needs rather than selfish. Can you imagine having to pay someone to teach you that?

I picked up the phone and dialed. My mom answered since my dad was out playing golf. There's no way to say something like this except to just come right out and say it, so that's what I did. All my life I'd tried to protect my mother from pain. I just didn't think she could cope. Well, the first thing my mother said after I told her I had cancer was, "Okay, let's not panic. What's the next thing we have to do?"

There were no hysterics, but rather a focused strength. She said she and my father would come out for the operation. I said we shouldn't decide anything until I spoke with the surgeon on Friday. Old habits die hard, but there I was not wanting them to have to cancel their already planned trip to visit my sister and the kids. I wish my dad had been home when I called. I don't know what my mom did or whom she dialed when she hung up from me, but I'm sure she experienced her own private hell.

After Leesa left for her next appointment, I called Elaine, who's always been there when I needed her and is like a second mother to me. Without skipping a beat she said, "Honey, I'm coming with you to the oncologist," and all I could say was, "Okay."

Then I called Rachel, who is, in my opinion, a brilliant woman, and she immediately zeroed in on the oncologist's name so she could cross-reference it with her own network of doctors. Rachel was particularly helpful in these circumstances because she herself is a survivor of a catastrophic neurological illness. If anyone knew how to navigate through the tough times ahead, it was her. She, too, said she'd go with me to the doctor's, and once again I said, "Okay." I swear, at another time I'd have been unable to say those two little syllables: *okay*.

When John came home, we hugged for a really long time. We kissed and made love. Slowly, gently, lovingly, as a tear rolled from the outer corner of my eye. He was exactly what the doctor ordered! I remembered my mom once telling me a story of a man who didn't want to have sex with his wife when she was diagnosed with a gynecological cancer, because he was afraid somehow he'd get the cancer, too. I'd always thought that was a selfish and uninformed way for a man to handle what was already a terrible situation.

John was beautiful and sensitive, though. I was overwhelmed by the tenderness and love I felt from him. Afterward, I realized I hadn't eaten, so we sought out a restaurant that was still serving lunch. I suggested going to the Ivy at the Shore in Santa Monica. There's a nice furniture store right next door and I'd been wanting to go there for some time.

John was obviously eager to do anything to lift my spirits, so we left the dog at home and ventured out. As we sat on the restaurant's terrace, I gazed out at the swaying palms and the Santa Monica pier just beyond. The Ferris wheel was turning, cars were honking, people were roller skating, and life seemed to be going on all around us.

This gal Anne, whom I'd socialized with several times, was just finishing up her lunch and popped by our table on her way out. She was very high energy and excited to see us, chatting up a storm about her job, her home, whatever. I can't even remember now. She was like a talking head. I could see her lips moving and I heard sound coming out of her mouth, but all I could think of was how surreal it all was, to be conversing as if everything were normal. She had no idea. Afterward, I blindly walked through the furniture store, muttering, "Purchase, I want to make a purchase." But I was unable to focus or make any decisions, so we got into the car and drove off.

John came up with an idea and started heading toward the freeway on-ramp. "Let's go into Beverly Hills and buy you that friendship ring we've been talking about," he exclaimed. Here it was June, and we'd been talking about this friendship ring since Valentine's Day. He hadn't known what to get me, and I said that I'd like something meaningful and everlasting like a friendship ring. No, I didn't make that up. Friendship rings are a real thing, made up by some other clever girl who wanted a ring from her man. For some reason the word *friendship* conjures up less fear than, let's say, *engagement* might.

Well, I'd seen something I liked while shopping at Barney's one day, and I liked a little platinum ring from the Tiffany's catalog as well. "Where should we go?" he asked. But I felt bad, like he was only suggesting this because he felt sorry for me and not because he truly wanted to. He insisted that he'd always intended on us going to pick out the friendship ring, but that a million things kept getting in the way. Now was the perfect time, and today was the perfect day. Who was I to argue? It was a lovely gesture.

So I called both stores to see how late they'd be open, because it was now around five in the afternoon and the shops in Beverly Hills tend to close early. As fate would have it, Barney's had just closed and Tiffany's was open another half hour. So Tiffany's it was!

As we drove from the beach to Beverly Hills in a race against the clock, I felt loved. We got to Tiffany's just as they were closing. I knew exactly what I wanted and they happened to have a ring that fit perfectly, a beautifully simple platinum-and-diamond Elsa Peretti friendship ring that I slipped on my thumb and haven't taken off since. As we drove home, I gazed down at my finger and contemplated my life. The future was uncertain and nothing made sense. I felt like a stranger in a strange land.

The First Night with Cancer

June 13, 2000

that evening when we got home, the house was empty and dimly lit by a night-light. Chester was asleep in the bedroom. As the sky darkened, so did the weight of the cancer. I walked around the house quietly, going through the motions of preparing for bed. The fish tank light illuminated the kitchen, John read in the living room, and I slipped into my bathroom to wash my face. Yup, "going through the motions" is a good way to describe it, because I was really somewhere else. Somewhere far away and deep inside my head. I opened a drawer, removed the toothpaste, turned on the faucet. I could see myself doing it all, but it all seemed strange, foreign, and out of step.

As I sat at my vanity, I thought about my things. My chair, my makeup, my toothbrush. *What will happen to them after I'm gone? Will they be trash for the garbage man to haul away? The toothbrush was expensive and I've got Lancôme I haven't even opened yet.* I felt myself plunging deeper and deeper into a horrible feeling of isolation. I was sitting there staring at my image, my face, *me,* when the piercing ring of the telephone broke through my silence. It was my sister, Nadine.

Now, my older sister and I have had a complicated relationship our whole lives. I say "older," but really we're only a year and eighteen days apart, a closeness in age that definitely exacerbated issues growing up. It's not easy being the "older" one when a baby comes into the house, especially when you're still a baby yourself. And since Nadine was always much taller than I, it made her seem even older. In fact, I never realized how close in age we really were until quite recently.

As an adult, being a year apart means nothing, but for us, as children, it created an enormous gap, each of us trying to define ourselves as individuals through friends, hobbies, sports, even food preferences. And everything seemed to be opposite. I was left-handed, she was right. I had dark hair, she had light. She liked athletics while I preferred performing arts.

As a teenager Nadine was always rebellious, which constantly worried my parents. In fact, for the better part of my life, I was either a witness or sounding board for my parents' endless worrying over my sister. In a desire not to give them any more cause for worry, or perhaps out of a competitive need to be the "good one," a lifelong pattern of self-denial, of not expressing my needs, of giving rather than taking, became my M.O.

Even as an adult, after I moved to California and was married to Peter, I hardly had a conversation with my mother that wasn't dominated by worries about my sister. First there was the issue that she wasn't married; then it was leaving her alone when my parents moved to Florida. These days, it's how hard she works while trying to raise two kids. It's always something, and because it's always been something, I think it prevented Nadine and I from experiencing the closeness I envied in other siblings.

Consequently, I'd never opened my eyes to see how much I had in common with her. We both were successful, career-driven women. We both loved to travel and hike. We both loved culture, theater, and museums. We loved restaurants, all different kinds of foods and entertaining. We could have been best friends, but unfortunately, that friendship we should have been sharing our entire lives was something we'd missed out on.

So it was my sister, Nadine, on the phone. Now, in all the time I was experiencing symptoms and searching for a diagnosis, I'd never once picked up the phone and reached out to her, an experienced nurse married to a doctor. What an idiot. How stupid of me, but asking for help wasn't in my vocabulary.

"How ya doin'?" she asked with concern.

"Ya know, I've been better," was all I could answer. I really didn't know how I was doing or what I was feeling, but I guess *numb* would have been a more appropriate answer.

"When do you see the surgeon?" She sounded businesslike.

"Um, Friday, not until Friday." I felt whipped, sapped of my strength.

"Did they grade the tumor, any mention of a letter or number?" She sounded like a nurse, my nurse.

"All she said was that it was very early, very slow growing, and very noninvasive." By soft-pedaling it, I hoped to convince myself it was hardly anything. The fact that it was indeed cancer was merely incidental. I still needed to be the *shtarkar,* the workhorse everyone else had come to depend on.

"Next time you talk to her, try to get a grade number, too," she said, as I wrote everything down on a list of things to remember to ask the surgeon on Friday.

"Okay," I answered.

"I'd also feel a lot better if the surgeon did her own biopsy." My sister was now in full medical mode. I'd never seen her in action before, and I regretted that I hadn't turned to her sooner.

"So I should tell her I want her to do another D&C?"

"Yes, definitely. The gynecologist took it in her office. Now you're working with a surgeon in a hospital. It's a more controlled environment, and I always like it when the surgeon starts fresh with her own tests. I think it's better." She was pretty insistent.

"All right, I'll tell her. I'm going to call her tomorrow and I'll tell her." I was glad my sister was now in the loop. She cared about me. She loved me, I could trust her to do right by me.

"Do you want Mom and Dad to cancel their trip to see me and the kids so they can be with you?" she asked. Did she know how hard a question that was for me to answer? I hemmed and hawed, then said, "Um, I don't know what I want." All I knew was, I didn't want to be the sick one, the weak one, the needy one. That was never my role, not in my entire life. Was I supposed to totally shift gears because of one call from my doctor?

"If you want them to come to you, they'll cancel their trip." Her voice began to escalate. "Is that what you want?"

"I don't want them to cancel their vacation. Let's see what happens," I answered, clearly in denial of the gravity of my situation.

"Fran, just say it. It's okay. If you want them to come, they'll come! Just say it!"

But I simply couldn't fit the words in my mouth. I've never asked anyone to sacrifice anything for me. I could take care of myself. "I want to wait until Friday, when I see the doctor," I answered, weakly. I just couldn't say what she wanted to hear, so she began to cry now, as well as scream.

"Why can't you just say it? You never just say what you want!"

But I couldn't and I didn't. Calmly and quietly I said, "Nadine, I just found out I had cancer today. I want to decide this on Friday, after I see the surgeon."

What she was expressing in all her rage was a lifetime of feelings that she hadn't ever voiced before. And she was right. I never said what I wanted, never asked for help, never let anyone in. I never opened up and shared my pain with anyone. And for everyone, but especially for my older sister, Nadine, that must have been an isolating hardship. Her voice instantly lowered and calmed. Though still filled with emotion, she became gentle and sympathetic.

"Okay, will you please call me if you need me?"

"I will."

"Any time of the day or night, I'm here for you."

"I know."

"I love you."

"I love you, too."

In that conversation, through my sister's fear and frustration, I saw myself as other people experience me, and I felt bad and inadequate as a friend, wife, daughter, and sister. John couldn't understand why she was yelling at me on the day I was diagnosed with cancer, but for the first time in my life I understood.

I went to bed, but I couldn't sleep. I was lucky I had both a mate and a dog. Neither one was ever really able to change anything for me, but there was a grounding factor to their presence. They were warm and loving and kept me from falling deep into my despair.

But when they were both sleeping and I was staring at the ceiling in solitude, my mind played tricks on me. And like the cemetery nightmare in *Fiddler on the Roof,* everything seemed to be leading me back to one conclusion: My days were numbered. The dog was aged. The marriage was over. My career had crescendoed with *The Nanny,* and in the silence of the night they all seemed to be nails in my coffin.

Why had I felt a recent urge to make out my will? Why had my favorite fish died? Why had I left Peter? Why had I told John he completed my life? Why? Why? Why? Because I must be about to *die!*

It all made so much sense. It was all over, now it was just a matter of time. I began to weep on my pillow, and as I sobbed John woke up. Bless his heart, he'd always wake out of a sound sleep to hold and comfort me. My thoughts were so loud in my head, but when I spoke, the words came out as whispers in the night, in the darkness, in my bed.

Panicked, I rattled off my hardly audible thoughts: "I think this must be it, maybe this is it. I'm scared, I'm scared, I'm scared. Was I bad, am I bad, is it because I hurt Peter, is that why this is happening?" But John whispered back that I was good, that he was there, and that we'd get through this.

In the morning he left for work and I called the surgeon, Doctor #9. Fuck it, I had to do something to gain some sense of control. "Why do I have to wait until Friday?" was my first question. Now that I knew I had cancer, every minute of every hour seemed like an eternity. I mean, what do you do with yourself? How do you pass the time when you know there's a cancer within you?

One good thing she said was that we didn't have to wait until we met on Friday to schedule an operating room. She said if I wanted her to, she could book me in for the following Wednesday. There was a room open and she was available. It was like scheduling a hair appointment instead of a hysterectomy. We all knew what I had, and that probably wasn't going to change, so the sooner we could get this tumor out of me the better. I told her to book the O.R. I was glad I'd called. If I hadn't, if I'd waited until my first appointment with her that Friday, my surgery might have been pushed even farther back. No sir, let them reserve the room for me, here and now. I figured I could always cancel if anything changed, but I can't get a room if it's already taken!

I told her my sister, the nurse, had said, "Get your surgeon to do her own biopsy."

"Fran, I'm happy to do whatever it takes to make you feel confident about the situation, but I just want you to know that the first thing I asked your gynecologist was, 'Are you sure this biopsy belongs to her, do the dates match, does the name match?' The tissue that was biopsied was you, Fran, definitely you. Plus, I also showed the tissue to my own pathologists to make doubly certain the report was correct. Again, I'm happy to satisfy your sister—as I said, whatever it takes, I understand you've been put through the wringer. But there's no doubt this is you, and you do have uterine cancer."

"Well, my sister said to do it, and I really think we should."

So even though I hadn't yet met my surgeon, the surgery was scheduled for Wednesday, June 21. I ultimately asked my parents to make the trip and they booked their flight for Tuesday. I alerted Ramon and Angelica to get the guest house ready. I wanted to be strong for what lay ahead, so I hiked; I wanted to feel confident, so I colored my hair; I needed to remain positive, so I saw my shrink. Oh, and I prayed. Man, did I pray. . . .

The Triple C Ranch

On Friday, Elaine picked up Rachel and met John and me at the special parking lot for cancer patients at Cedars. John brought a pad and pen for notes. I wore some cool pants and a tie-dyed top I'd bought in London. As we walked down the hospital hallways, I looked so healthy I felt like I didn't belong there. Paintings and sculptures lined the walls, a much-appreciated distraction.

A strained cheerfulness sifted through our chitchat as we rode the elevator to the lower level where I'd meet the surgeon, Doctor #9, for the first time. We were instructed to go straight to the nurses' station, past a magnificent saltwater aquarium that sat in a prominent position in the waiting area, another well-chosen touch of beauty and grace in an otherwise abysmal destination. The room was filled with somber people and their somber families, each experiencing their own kind of misery. The most heartbreaking were the children.

All the nurses recognized me right away as I was ushered into an examining room that included a wall of chairs and a curtain that, when drawn, would divide the room in two. Rachel talked about the twins, her toddlers, as Elaine held up her compact and applied her lipstick.

Three different women, each with a task, entered the room. One took my blood pressure, one took my temperature, and one took my pulse. I knew they all wanted to gawk at me because I was the Nanny. Surely other people don't have a separate nurse just to take their temperature. It was inappropriate and made me feel self-conscious. Didn't they realize I had cancer? But I guess they were all just too excited to meet the Nanny and couldn't help themselves.

One by one the nurses voiced their love for the show and expressed how much they missed it. Each shared an anecdote about a child or a parent who was particularly devoted. They all commented on how much younger I looked in person than on TV, which I could have taken as ass-kissing, but opted not to. It's a strange paradox being treated like a star when on another level you're actually a cancer patient. I didn't know how to respond. And even though I didn't like it, I didn't blame them, either.

A short time later, after removing my shoes, jewelry, and belt, I still weighed in at close to 140. "Why do hospitals always have 'fat' scales?" I joked halfheartedly as the nurse pushed the metal balance farther and farther to the right. I wondered how much a woman's reproductive organs weigh and how much thinner I'd be after the surgery.

Then two other nurses, Lucy and Wanda, who seemed to work directly with my surgeon, arrived. They were extremely pleasant both in appearance and personality. If I were a surgeon, the first thing I'd look for in a nurse after her qualifications would be a good bedside manner. It makes such a difference in your experience.

On the other hand, personality *shouldn't* be the deciding factor in which doctor becomes your surgeon. The way I see it, most surgeons are in a personality class all their own. Doing precision work with a knife doesn't call for the same tact or charm a non-surgeon must display in meeting, greeting, and comforting patients on a daily basis. When it comes to surgery, get the best in the field and forget about the rest. You're not looking for a date or a potential spouse. You're never going to go to the movies together or out to dinner. What you need—the *only* thing you need—is someone who's good with a knife. Period.

When Doctor #9 entered, we were all surprised at how young and attractive she was, considering the level she'd reached in her field. She pulled herself together really well: Armani suit, Chanel shoes, makeup, hair, and nails all done to a T. *This is my surgeon?* I thought. She looked more like a studio executive. Elaine, who was the oldest and I guess the one Doctor #9 appeared youngest to, exclaimed out loud that she "couldn't believe how young and gorgeous" she was.

It was true: Out of the many doctors I'd seen, she made by far the best presentation. A feather in her cap, I'd say. John took out his pad and pen to take notes, titling the page "Sweetie's Visit to the Triple C Ranch" (short for "Cedars Cancer Center"). The first and most shocking statement Doctor #9 made was how terrible it was that it had taken this long to diagnose me. She couldn't understand why *none* of the previous doctors thought to do a D&C.

"What I teach all my students, and what everybody learns in med school, is: bleeding between periods, biopsy. Period. What happens between medical school and practice I'll never know!" That's exactly what she said; I'll never forget her directness. She added that, based on my menstrual history, I was probably suffering from something called luteal phase defect. *Luteal WHAT?* I had a defect that no one knew about?

Probably from as early as my very first period, she theorized, I'd always run low on progesterone, and if there's one thing the uterus hates more than anything, it's what's called unopposed estrogen.

That's when you have too much, or even normal amounts of, estrogen, but it's not balanced or countered by the appropriate amounts of progesterone. I'd always had extremely short cycles (nineteen to twenty-four days, tops), and the one and only time I accidentally got pregnant, I began to miscarry immediately. I was in my late teens, already with Peter. I'd just had my period and thought it would be okay not to use a condom. Whoops. At the time I didn't dwell on the implications of my inability to carry the pregnancy forward. I was simply relieved not to be confronted with a difficult decision. Had I seriously tried to have a baby in my twenties or even my thirties, I might have been diagnosed with the hormone imbalance years before, because I probably wouldn't have been able to go full term. Instead, the condition caused the glands in my uterine wall to rebel and grow a malignant ball the size of a walnut.

I felt anger toward the medical community and the doctors I'd seen prior to Doctor #9, including Doctor #8. Even though she ultimately was the one who diagnosed me, she should have given me the D&C right away. Why didn't she test me for uterine cancer before treating me for a perimenopausal condition I didn't have? Why assume it's one thing when you haven't ruled out another?

The surgeon, while snapping on her rubber gloves, bluntly added, "Politicians and celebrities get the worst medical treatment. Who wants to stick their thumb up the ass of the president and tell him he's got cancer?"

Well, no one really knew how to respond to that one, so there was a general wave of nodding until I blurted out the incongruous remark, "That's how Elvis died!" Which got no reaction at all. This was the first time a connection had been made between my fame and the lack of a diagnosis. I hadn't thought of it before, but there it was right under my nose. Right in her office with those nurses. *Can anyone be thorough in their job when they're completely distracted by celebrity?* I wondered.

The next thing ya know, we're on to colonoscopies. I wasn't thrilled with the idea of having a camera shoved up my butt, but I knew I wanted one and had mentioned it to her when we first spoke on the phone. My stool had changed in recent months, but the closest thing I could get to a diagnosis was my internist's telling me I was eating too much spinach.

My dad's older sister, Rosalind, a dear aunt of mine, had died from ovarian cancer that eventually spread to her colon. As years go by it's difficult to differentiate between diagnostic fact and family folklore, but that's what I believed to be true. My fear was that my cancer had been diagnosed too late and might have spread like hers.

The surgeon had no problem with scheduling a colonoscopy, and repeated again and again that she was willing to do anything I wanted for me to finally feel like I was in the right hands. A gastrointestinal specialist, Doctor #10, would perform the procedure the day before my surgery. That way I wouldn't have to take the barium, which clears out your intestines, more than once.

With great fanfare Wanda drew the curtain to separate me from John, Elaine, and Rachel as the exam was about to begin. She held my hand as Lucy and the surgeon did another D&C on me, this time sans Novocain. Though Doctor #9 still felt the second biopsy wasn't necessary, she wanted to gain my trust by accommodating my sister's request. She even took my sister's work number at the hospital to fill her in on everything. Doctor #9 really went to great lengths to rectify the damage that had been done by her colleagues. Meanwhile, she seemed to be going to town down there, snipping away tiny chunks of tissue that Lucy gingerly dropped into a vial for biopsy. Man, did that hurt. Thank God it only lasted a minute.

While Lucy helped me clean up and get dressed, Doctor #9 moved to the other side of the curtain to talk to Rachel, John, and Elaine. "This will be a piece of cake," she said. "The gynecologist's biopsy indicated the tumor was a baby cancer, just beginning to turn malignant. It's one hundred percent curable."

We all left feeling encouraged and good about my surgeon. It was a relief that it was over. John left for work while Elaine, Rachel, and I went out to lunch. As we ate and drank and tried to remain optimistic, I couldn't stop thinking about those patients in the waiting room. The sadness in their faces, the thinness of their bodies, the baldness of their heads. Would that be me? Is that where I was headed? I didn't want to go there at all, so I rejoined the conversation in progress: babies, vacations, the menu. When the waiter walked by, I ordered another glass of wine.

"Now I'm Concerned"

O ver the weekend I worked with John writing our MTV pilot. I remember awakening during the night in one of my scared moments of tears and whispers, begging him to finish the script with me. "Who knows what's going to happen? This may be our last chance to complete it." I wanted to see his idea become a teleplay. I hated the idea that I might be leaving this earth with an unfinished piece of work. So with the weight of an uncertain future resting squarely on my shoulders, we pulled out the laptop and attempted to write a comedy. And I'm grateful we did, because it was fun to return to our make-believe world. I thought it romantic, the notion we were creating a place no one else knew about but us. It was an escape from reality I welcomed.

I also prepared the guest house for my parents' arrival, and continued to hike as well. When Monday rolled around, John left for work and I geared my day around the barium I was to drink that afternoon in preparation for the colonoscopy on Tuesday. My dad had had one recently and said it was nothing. I thought it strange that everything I was getting, my mom or dad had also recently gotten. They were able to share their experiences with me, guiding me with firsthand knowledge. It was like I was a child again, a big 140-pound baby—something I hadn't allowed myself to be in a long time.

Rachel and her husband, Greg, made plans to come out to the beach and have lunch with me before I had to take the barium drink. After that, I'd only be able to have liquids or Jell-O until I came through the surgery on Wednesday. It was a beautiful day, the sun was glistening on the ocean, and I made a reservation at Geoffrey's, a restaurant on a cliff overlooking the Pacific. I always feel like I'm in Hawaii when I go there, and I thought Rachel and Greg would enjoy dining alfresco by the sea.

We talked about poor Nancy Marchand dying of lung cancer. Not too morbid while having a little lunch. How wonderful for her she got to play such a great part on such a landmark television series as *The Sopranos* all the way up to the end. I saw her perform off-Broadway in *The Cocktail Hour,* and always loved her after that.

I was glad I'd done *The Nanny*. It made me feel successful in my career goals. What would be my next part? *Would* there be a next part? I ordered the fish, grilled crispy over spinach and whipped potatoes. Usually I like pasta, but this sounded good. Greg and I had wine; Rachel never drinks. We raised our glasses and toasted to it all going well, and all being over on Wednesday.

As we all got back in my car and headed home, I called for my messages on the cell phone. The nurse had left a message saying that the surgeon had more information from the most recent biopsy (the one my sister had insisted on) and would like me to stop by her office before going in for my colonoscopy tomorrow. That's as much as I heard before the phone went dead and I was stuck in a cellular void of no reception for the rest of the way home. Now, it couldn't have been more than ten minutes, tops, but I felt my entire piece of salmon get stuck in my chest as I frantically kept trying to get a signal so I could connect with the nurse.

When Greg, Rachel, and I arrived at the house, Angelica and Ramon were still there. "Fran, how many minutes can you record on your video camera?" Ramon asked as I entered the kitchen.

"I don't know, forty?" I guessed as I dialed the nurse on my hard line. Ramon and his timing, always with the obtuse questions. It's part of his charm, I guess.

Rachel tried to ground the situation with simple logic: "Whatever it is, we'll just deal with it, that's all."

I remembered I had to take the barium drink. Greg, otherwise known as "the bartender from hell," prepared it. When I got through to the nurse, she simply repeated the message she'd already left, but I dug in my heels and said, "I'm sorry, but there's no way I will be able to wait until tomorrow to find out what this new information is!" She explained that Doctor #9 was in surgery all day.

"I don't care!" I answered, with panic in my voice. "Can't she call me on her way from one operation to the other?" It seemed unfathomable to wait. I mean, how torturous. She said the doctor would be coming out in a few minutes and she'd try to get her to call then.

Rachel said, "We'll wait with you."

"Are you sure? I mean, I know you probably should be getting back to the kids," I said, feeling like a burdensome pain.

"Don't be ridiculous, the kids are fine. We're not leaving," she insisted. Once again, I was learning something valuable: When those around you offer to help carry the load, take it for the lifesaver it is and simply say *thank you*. So we all went into my bedroom and played with Chester. That dog was so intelligent and plugged in to me, he sensed right away something was wrong and anxiously awaited the surgeon's call along with the rest of us.

Well, just as I was massaging Chester's little old bones (he was now eighteen years old) and listening to Rachel tell a story, the phone rang. We all froze. Rachel stopped talking, Angelica stopped folding laundry, and I grabbed the receiver. It was Doctor #9.

I picked up my notepaper and pen from the side of the bed as Rachel and Greg held their breath. There was no small talk, no pussyfooting around, no soft-pedaling. She came right out and said, "I'm glad we listened to your sister because the second biopsy shows a more advanced cancer than the first."

"What do you mean, 'more advanced'?" I said. I looked up at Rachel, who was hanging on every word.

She explained that a more extensive scraping of the uterine tissue indicated not only cells that were grades of one and two, but also threes and fours.

My head was whirling. Thank God for Nadine. The request she made for a second biopsy might have seemed like overkill at the time, but proved to be one of the single greatest pieces of advice I'd received from a medical professional throughout this whole unfortunate mess. How could this be happening? "What does that mean exactly?" I asked, always trying to understand and write down everything she said.

"Well, before, it appeared to be what I think of as a baby cancer, where the cells are just beginning to turn, but to now find cells that are grades three and four—I gotta be honest with you, Fran, now I'm concerned."

I'll never forget those three words: *now I'm concerned*. A malignant tumor can have cells in it varying in grades from one through four (four being the worst). Which grade of cells dominates determines what grade the tumor is. If it's a grade-four tumor, suffice it to say, you're in pretty bad shape.

"I'm going to want to do a radical hysterectomy. That means you'll have to lose your ovaries and I won't be able to perform the surgery laparoscopically or vaginally; we'll have to cut into the abdomen."

Rachel held my hand. She knew from the look on my face I was devastated. I don't know what made me think of this right then—maybe it had been in the back of my head all along—but I said, "I want to freeze my ovaries just in case they're disease-free. Maybe I could harvest the eggs someday." And then I added, "I'm going to want a plastic surgeon to sew me up, too."

She still thought surgery would essentially cure me, since uterine cancer is pretty noninvasive and slow growing. In that respect I was lucky. Even though as a young, thin woman I was atypical for uterine cancer (it mostly affects postmenopausal or obese women), out of all the gynecological cancers I could have gotten, this was the best—"best" meaning least likely to spread if caught early. There I was, *finally* too young and thin for something, and I get it anyway.

"But," she explained, "with all cancers, we never know what stage it's at until the surrounding tissue and lymph nodes are removed and biopsied. How deep and how far-reaching the cancer has gone will determine what stage of the disease you have."

Meanwhile, I'd read somewhere that uterine cancer was the only gynecological cancer with a mortality rate that was on the rise, in part due to late diagnosis. So there you are.

I hung up the phone and wept in Rachel's arms. "I think it's better they take everything anyway," Rachel said. That's what we call being Talmudic about life. "What do you need it for? Get it all out and be done with it, be clean of it."

I called my mom again, who was busy getting ready for their flight to L.A. on Tuesday, and told her this unexpected plot twist. She was in full agreement with Rachel. "Get it the hell outta ya," were her exact words. She'd never felt comfortable with the surgeon's doing a partial hysterectomy anyway. The radical seemed more thorough, more efficient. Let's hope so, anyway, because that's what I was getting. Thanks to my sister, we were all better prepared. Not only was the surgeon better able to judge the type of surgery I needed, but I'd now go under the knife knowing exactly what to expect.

I reached Elaine on her cell phone at a charity event. "Oh Elaine," I wept. "They got the results back from the biopsy and it's much more advanced than the surgeon thought. I think it's time we tell Peter." Up until this point I really hadn't wanted to worry him. He was so far away, and had gone through so much already, not only with the divorce but with having lost both his parents to cancer years before. I'd been thinking I'd write him a letter after it was all done, but things had changed. The situation seemed graver, and I worried that the news might leak to the press. I didn't want him to find out that way, so I asked Elaine, as one of our oldest friends and faithful manager, to please tell him.

From her charity event, in the hotel parking lot in an evening gown, she called Peter on her cell phone. He began to cry immediately, she later told me. All the anger melted away and what was left, all that was left, was the love. He told her to tell me that he knew about John and understood, but if I needed him, he'd jump on the next flight out and be by my side through it all. When Elaine called me back and relayed his message, I cried like a baby. It was the sweetest expression of love we'd shared in years, one of many silver linings to come.

When the phone rang again, it was John returning my 911 page for the second time in less than a week. With fear in his voice he said, "Are you okay? What's the matter?" I told him the cancer was worse and the surgery would be more radical. He said he'd leave work immediately. He was never to return to the job again.

As for me, I felt sick to my stomach, and ran to the bathroom. The barium had kicked in. . . .

The Night Before

i n my heart I feared life would never be normal again once the surgery was performed, and I suddenly had a great need to spend as many last minutes as possible in my home by the sea with my beloved dog, Chester. It sounds calming, but actually my house is pretty chaotic, always full of life, with friends, barking dogs, and workers. It's a bit of a zoo, but it's *my* zoo, and I wanted to wrap it in my arms and never let go.

My sister told me to make sure the hospital knew who my designated partner was going to be. I wanted it to be John. He'd be the last person I'd see in pre-op and the first person I'd see in post-op. Funny how important and significant my relationship with John had become in such a brief time. After two and a half decades with Peter, a lifetime with my parents, and twenty years of friendship with Elaine, as well as Judi and Rachel, it was John whom I needed, whom I wanted.

John is a natural caregiver. It's surprising how similar we are in this respect. His need to make everyone happy relates to an older brother's having died of crib death years before John was born. As he grew up, he was told over and over again that he was the miracle God gave the family to make everything better and take all the pain away. How's that for pressure? And I, of course, needed to make everyone happy because I felt guilty that my mother almost died giving birth to me. It's because of our history that we both always shift into rescue mode. "I'll fix, I'll make better, I'll handle things." Such is our lot in life!

Normally, I won't let him feel responsible for me and vice versa. But now was different. I let him make it all about me. I could relax completely around him; John would be strong for the both of us. And thank God for him, because I was really worried about the colonoscopy. My aunt's cancer had spread to the colon. Everyone used to say we looked alike. I was so scared that my fate was linked to hers. Especially after having been told that my cancer was more advanced, I felt sure it must have spread. But Elaine told me to put a rubber band around my wrist and snap it each time I'd start thinking terrible thoughts. *Ouch*. It hurt when I did that, and I think the pain distracted me. "Don't mix fear with imagination," she'd say. "It's a deadly cocktail!" And she was right. But try as I might, it was difficult not to, because once I was told I had cancer, anything seemed possible.

Going to the hospital for the colonoscopy was like a dress rehearsal for the surgery on Wednesday. Doctor #10 told us they'd insert a long tube through the rectum all the way into the intestines to see if there were any growths. Yikes. It all sounded so gross. I can't believe people actually go into that field. I was put under heavy sedation through an I.V. and didn't feel a thing. My doctor had also given both Elaine and her husband, Allan, colonoscopies. This same little man had looked up all three of our asses. Eww. Whatta business!

Anyway, much to my relief, when I awakened from the sedation, the doctor told me I was totally clean; he saw no growths of any kind. What a great guy. No wonder Elaine and Allan love him so much. We'll never bend over for anyone but him!

This hospital treats many high-profile celebrities and has a V.I.P. department that deals with the special needs that go along with fame. So after the colonoscopy, we met the V.I.P. rep. She was a pleasant, well-dressed, amiable woman who made us feel very welcome and seemed quite confident that the hospital would be able to keep my condition under wraps. As she swept through the corridors pointing out back doors and hidden hallways, she said, "Every staff member of our hospital signs a confidentiality clause in their work contract. Tomorrow, we'll register you under an alias, I'll meet you at a side entrance, and every effort will be made to protect your privacy."

"But when my girlfriend Twiggy underwent surgery here, they told her the same thing, and still it was leaked to the tabloids," I challenged. I mean, I didn't want to sound difficult, but they did give Twiggy the same spiel.

"That was the *British* tabloids," she said dismissively, as though that was supposed to make me feel better.

"But still, someone at the hospital must have leaked the story," I said.

"Who knows?" she said, pointing out the beautiful view from what would soon be my hospital room. "Try to worry less about that and more about getting better."

What was there to say? My only hope was that I'd emphasized my concerns sufficiently that every precautionary measure would be taken. My girlfriend Donna once said, "You won't believe how much time and effort is spent trying to ensure your privacy." She and her husband, Danny, have spent the better part of their adult lives dodging the press, and now I was in the same boat. I'd never thought I'd get to this point, but every celebrity does, eventually.

When Peter and I first started *The Nanny,* we enjoyed the press and their fascination with our having been high-school sweethearts. It was a Hollywood fairy tale of sorts. Two kids from humble beginnings in Queens, New York, meet, fall in love, and move to California to pursue their dreams of making it in show biz. In the show's early years it helped to do as much press as possible, and so Peter and I were both amenable. But we'd painted ourselves into a corner that nobody could possibly have predicted. Unless of course you were somebody who'd been there, done that, and paid dearly for it.

The very people who wrote such nice things about us in the early days were the most venomous after our breakup. It was horrible, but I had to learn the hard way. I finally understood why Danny and Donna had eloped. They knew what I lived to find out: that it's best to be as low profile as possible, because the press's appetite is unending. Papers and magazines need content every day of every month of every year after year after year. . . .

When I moved out of our home in Hancock Park, reporters were all over both of us. They camped out on our front lawn and harassed Peter constantly. Stalkerazzi sat in cars outside my apartment and followed me in my car. I'd been paired in the tabloids with everyone from my assistant to Danny to Esa-Pekka Salonen, the resident conductor of the Los Angeles Philharmonic. If I was simply seen shaking the hand of someone it was cause for gossip. Peter and I had unwittingly set up the feeding frenzy by exploiting our once happy relationship for the benefit of the show. I wouldn't ever do that again, not in a million years.

We returned home to the beach by midafternoon and beat the rush-hour traffic. Dear, sweet Angelica prepared a big bowl of orange Jell-O for my return. The new coffee table and my beautiful Botero in all her zaftig bronze glory were a welcoming sight. Life continued to go on all around me despite my own personal horror. And I suppose it was good in a way that it did, because it helped pull me out of the nightmare and gave me things to talk about besides the nasty business of cancer.

My friend Caryn and I had been keeping close tabs on the

Lakers' NBA finals. We thought they'd win in five, but it was the sixth game against the Pacers that won them the trophy. While we worried and grieved over my now more advanced case of cancer, the rest of Los Angeles was rejoicing over the Lakers' first championship in twelve years. Gotta love that Shaq!

When Tuesday night rolled around and my folks arrived, they were thrilled to see how well I looked. I don't know what they were expecting, but I had to admit, I did look good, and we were all grateful the colonoscopy was normal. I was thrilled to feel their arms around me as we all hugged at once. Each time they expressed how great I looked, I'd return the compliment, because they really did look so healthy, vibrant, and well. But I know that their words to me were more than complimentary; they were an expression of profound relief.

"What are ya cooking? Do I smell garlic?" my mom asked while sniffing the air.

"I'm making shrimp scampi over linguine for you guys and John," I answered, knowing that was one of their favorites. "I can't eat until after the operation."

"We're not hungry," my dad chimed in. "Mother made us each two sandwiches for the plane, one peanut butter, one tuna fish," he added. She hates when he calls her "Mother," but for some reason when he's around the kids he goes into automatic "Mother" mode. He just can't help himself.

"I packed us a lunch because they'd only give us breakfast on the plane," she explained.

"And it's a good thing we did because not two hours later we got hungry again, and ate the sandwiches for lunch," Dad said while lifting the lid off the shrimp.

They'd flown American Airlines nonstop from Florida to L.A. that day. "It was one of the nicest flights we've ever been on," Mom said, mushing Chester into her bosom. After a brief tour of whatever new stuff I'd done with the house, we all sat around the dinner table.

"We're not even hungry," Mom said.

"We're hardly gonna eat a thing," Dad added, as he began shoveling in the pasta. My one regret was that I'd made only a pound of linguine, because there wasn't enough for seconds or leftovers.

"I love pasta!" my dad exclaimed as he used his fork to twirl up the lion's share of the pound.

"Linguine with shrimp scampi and plenty of garlic is my favorite," my mom said while pushing the last strand on her fork with her thumb. I've said it before and I'll say it again: The Dreschers are good eaters!

I bought a WebTV for my dad to play with. I thought it would be fun for us to e-mail each other, and helpful for them to have the Internet for travel or medical research at their fingertips. He didn't open the box, but decided he'd save it until he got back to Florida. "I wouldn't want to interfere with Mother's TV viewing," he said and then shifted to his favorite subject, Tiger Woods, who'd just won the U.S. Open. "He's the greatest golfer who ever lived!" Dad shouted, as he swung an imaginary nine-iron in the living room.

Mom thought Chester looked well, even though I'd nicknamed him Mr. Wobbly at this point, because of his difficulty standing and walking. It's true; he was still a beautiful dog. I was glad the show had ended and I'd been able to spend more time caring for him in his later years. My mom thought I should write a children's book about Mr. Wobbly, who thought he died and went to heaven in my beautiful white home. Don't ask me why this struck her as such a hot seller, but she repeated it a few times until I finally said, "Why don't *you* write it, Mom?" And that was the end of it. They're both really creative, my parents, but they never seem to get past the idea stage. Under the circumstances it all seemed pretty normal.

As we kissed each other good night, I remembered another Elaine wisdom: "Plan your play, then play your plan." Well, the plan was to undergo the surgery, get it over with, and then everything would return to being like it used to be. Feeble as it was, at least we had a plan.

That night I didn't sleep well at all. I mean, I have trouble sleeping the night before I'm getting on a flight to go on vacation; can you imagine preparing to go in for cancer surgery? It bothered me that my dad hadn't opened his present. I tossed and turned all night, running a dialogue over and over in my head. I knew he hadn't meant anything by it, but I worried that it wouldn't be good for me to go under the knife with unresolved anger.

It was still quite early in the morning as I lay in bed staring up at the ceiling while John slept. I wish I slept as soundly as him. Even under the best of circumstances I'm never able to stay asleep for as long or as late as he does. This morning was no different, so I crept into my bathroom and dialed my parents. I knew they'd be up because they were still on East Coast time and my mother and I share the same sleep habits, which means she probably hadn't slept a wink.

She answered, and we commiserated about the lousy night we'd had. I didn't have to be at the hospital until early afternoon, and we discussed going in two cars so they could return at the end of the day to be with Chester. John would remain with me but still have a car at the hospital in case he needed to run out for something over the course of my stay. I guess I should say "our" stay, since he'd decided to remain with me the whole time.

I asked to speak with my dad, so Mom put him on. Poor guy didn't know what was coming, but I'd worked myself up over this WebTV gift, fueled by my anxiety and anguish over my illness. I wasn't taking shit from nobody! "I'd really like you to set up the WebTV so we can write to each other," I said bluntly.

But Dad wasn't catching my drift and answered, "I'm gonna set it up just as soon as we get back to Florida." *Oy*, he could be so dense sometimes.

"I want you to set it up here, first, so we can use it together while I recover," I replied.

Of course he just couldn't see the necessity of it all and responded, "But Mother loves to watch her programs on the TV." Now, this just got me so incensed I saw red.

"Why can't you just open it and set it up? There are two TVs, and besides, she doesn't watch TV twenty-four hours a day," I continued. "She reads her novels, she talks to her mother, she takes her time doing her hair and putting on makeup. Can't we ever share in anything without you making it about Mom?" I'm sure he wasn't sensitive to how he was making me feel, but the time had come to let him know.

There was an episode of *The Nanny* that dealt with this very subject. Miss Fine got some tickets to a sporting event for herself and her father, thinking he'd be so happy, but she was mistaken; he chose to watch the game on TV.

I'd directed that episode since it held deep and personal meaning for me. The story had been inspired by a similar experience I'd had with my dad when I was able to score two impossible-to-get basketball tickets for us. He turned me down because he didn't want to leave my mother out. Attending the game would have meant only three or four hours out of his day. I don't know whether he doesn't like to be alone with me, or whether he uses her as his excuse for stuff he doesn't want to do, or whether he's just so into her that there's no room for anyone else, but stuff like that always made me feel like a third wheel.

I was really quite pathetic. Crying, while pleading with him to please open the box and set up the damn thing. My dad is so sweet and loving, but he can be unwittingly insensitive. "Okay, sweetie," he finally said. "I hear where you're coming from, and I *will* set it up. In fact, I'm gonna go read the instructions right now! Okay, darling?" Bless his heart.

Well, all the screaming and crying drove John out of bed, as well as Chester. It was official, the day had begun. Ramon and Angelica began cleaning up the dishes from the night before. "Fran, have you ever gone scuba diving? What's it like?" Ramon asked.

"Yes, Ramon. But I didn't like it, it hurt my ears," I answered, while putting on my hiking boots.

"Oh, the ears. I never thought of that," he mumbled. I wanted to take a walk. One last walk before going in for the surgery. I thought of stories I'd heard of people who'd been in terrible accidents, but because they were in such strong condition, they survived where others might have perished. Tony Danza was one of those people. When he got into that near-fatal skiing accident, everyone said he would have been dead if it weren't for his having once been a professional boxer and having retained a hard physique.

I hoped the stronger my body was, the faster I'd recover. I love being out in nature and I wanted to be in as Zen a place as possible. I actually felt so much better now that I'd cleared the air with my dad. To this day I don't really know if he indulged me because I had cancer and was going in for the surgery or because he realized I had a legitimate beef. My therapist would say it was probably a little bit of both.

Anyway, John, Chester, and I got into the car and were heading for my favorite trail when I suddenly thought of an even more perfect spot. I felt a strong and powerful calling to head to a retreat for Franciscan monks I knew high atop a beautiful mountain overlooking the ocean. It has tranquil gardens with fountains and quiet spots to sit and meditate. You have to park your car at the bottom and hike up to the top, but a small slice of paradise awaits those who do. I've always loved Saint Francis of Assisi because he was the saint who loved all the little animals. Whenever you see a statue of him, you'll often spot a bird or two resting on his shoulders.

I carried Chester in my arms—his walking days were long over—and the three of us made our way up to the top. I was in tremendous shape, and the climb presented little challenge, but the exhilaration of being there made me positively euphoric.

A German Shepherd puppy, maybe six months old, greeted us on our approach. His tag said his name was Joe and he was the sweetest, friendliest pup. Who wouldn't be if he lived in Shangri-la? He stayed with us the whole time during our visit. It was refreshing to be around such a happy, gawky young dog. John, Chester, and I all really enjoyed his attention. He was pure innocence, there was no heaviness to him like there was with us. He was like an angel in a heavenly place.

As we sat on a bench at the base of the Saint Francis statue overlooking all the coastline below us, I turned to John and said, "I don't wanna go." He looked at me with strength and compassion and said, "I know, Franny, but you gotta go." And of course he was right, I *had* to go. We petted, kissed, and hugged Joe like departing dear old friends. He followed us a ways down the hill but connected with a groundskeeper who brought him back up to the retreat.

Without words we got back in the car and drove home. Methodically, I put a few things in a bag to take to the hospital. What do you take? Nothing of value, but things that would bring me comfort and remind me of home. I grabbed a picture of Chester, a stuffed teddy bear, a pewter dolphin John had bought me, some sundries, a book, and pajamas.

I got down on the floor and stroked Chester, knowing if anything happened to me, Kathryn would take care of him the way he was used to. She's the gal who works closest with me on all of my affairs, and over the years has proved as much a friend as coworker. He loved Kathryn, and she loved him.

As I walked through the house, Angelica, with tears in her eyes, hugged me long and fully and whispered, "Good luck, Fran." When I got into the car in the garage, Ramon came running over to the window. I wondered what he was going to ask me this time, but much to my amazement he leaned into the car, hugged me, and said softly, "We love you, Fran. You are not alone."

The Surgery

June 21, 2000

I'd never been given anesthesia before. Even at the dentist, I'd never received gas for the fillings, and the thought of it really scared me. During my formative years, my mom felt compelled to share endless neighborhood horror stories. Right before my surgery, I remembered one of these stories. There I was, no more than twelve, eating Rice Krispies at the breakfast table minding my own business, when my mother entered.

"Ya know Richie, the lifeguard at the pool club?" she asked casually, while pouring some juice.

"Yes," I answered innocently, unsuspecting of the tragic tale about to unfold.

"Well, he had a girlfriend, Marsha Rifkin's daughter. Ya know Marsha Rifkin?" she asked, as she popped a Geritol vitamin in her mouth.

"No," I said, trying to hear my "snap, crackle, and pop."

"Very short, kinda chubby."

"No."

"Sure you do," she insisted. "She always wears wedgies, very big breasts . . ."

"Oh yeah," I cut her off, just to end this litany of description.

"Well, anyway, her daughter used to date Richie and she was a beautiful girl, *much* prettier than the girl he's going out with now," she said, pouring herself a mug of coffee.

"So?" I said, playing with the mound of milky sugar at the bottom of my Tupperware bowl.

"Well, she went in for knee surgery. Nothing important, no big deal," she said, while ripping open a Sweet'N Low. I could feel my throat begin to tighten, anticipating the ill-fated end of Marsha Rifkin's poor, pretty daughter.

"What happened?" Like roadkill, I didn't want to know, but I had to find out.

"She died," Mom said, stirring her coffee for dramatic emphasis.

I immediately thought of poor Richie the lifeguard, and felt sad. "How? Why?" Sour milk came up in my throat.

"She was allergic to the anesthesia!" There was always a big payoff to Mom's stories. Before that moment, I'd never known something like that was even possible. And then my mother added, as if that weren't enough, "Yup. She never got off the table! Drink ya juice."

Hearing this at such an impressionable age left an everlasting fear of going under anesthesia. Certainly any *elective* surgery that would require it was always completely out of the question. There I was about to enter a hospital, have major surgery, and go under anesthesia for the first time. Needless to say, I was pretty nervous. Who was the anesthetist? Was he any good? What kind of anesthesia was I going to get? How much or how little and for how long?

Both my mom and dad had recently undergone some much more minor and less invasive surgery than I, which involved their being put under, and they came through it with flying colors, so I felt somewhat comforted. Of course, I was the only one of the three to get cancer, but I chose to ignore that minor detail.

I asked my parents what they were given and found out it was the same thing as me, the most commonly administered anesthetic. That calmed me, but I still spoke to everyone anyway. Were they prepared for an allergic reaction? Did they know I tend to have a low threshold for most drugs? Would they administer the minimum first? I'm sure they thought I was a pain in the ass, but meanwhile, I was the one going under the knife!

Upon my arrival at the hospital I was informed that I'd need a chest X ray. Well, that just opened up a whole new can of worms! I hate X rays, and have them only when absolutely necessary. Even when I go to the dentist, I'm reluctant to get X rays, which many dentists consider routine. Now, I could be totally off base on this, but I don't need to help my dentist pay for his expensive X ray machine. Let's not forget, it's a business, and they do have overhead. Meanwhile, you're the one getting radiated. No thank you.

I asked the nurse why, if I was getting a hysterectomy, I needed a chest X ray. "It's standard hospital procedure," she said. "No patient can be admitted without one."

John looked at me and said, "Take the X ray. What are you gonna do?"

So I had myself a small conniption, and then begrudgingly said, *"Fine,"* as I started to unbutton my shirt.

As previously arranged in an effort to keep my illness a secret, I was admitted under a different name to ensure maximum privacy. I had enough to worry about—I mean, I had cancer, for God's sake!—and the last thing I wanted was to have my nightmare turned into a media circus. I'd already paid the price of fame. When my life was falling apart, my heart was breaking, and my world was coming to an end, the press didn't care, because to them I was just a headline.

The day of the surgery I told my parents, who'd acquired some level of notoriety themselves through their appearances as Early Bird restaurant critics on *The Rosie O'Donnell Show,* that they should try to keep a low profile when at the hospital. I told them to say as little as possible. "Ma, ya don't need to be showing the parking attendant our family photos," I whined. They're so innocent, proud, and friendly, it's difficult for them to be tight-lipped. It's simply not in their makeup, I suppose.

I feel bad that my paranoia was so focused on them, but they just seemed like the wild cards I couldn't control. I don't know why I got so nervous about it all, but I did. I think psychologically, I felt so out of control where my body was concerned, I must have had some need to at least try to control the press situation. I also think I was still in denial of my cancer, still wanting to quietly put it behind me without everyone finding out, especially within the biz.

So anyway, there I was, under an alias, checked in and off to pre-op. I was told to get undressed and put on a hospital gown. I kept on my sweat socks and even then I tried to look nice, still wearing a little lipstick and blush. They made me remove the engagement—uh, I mean *friendship*—ring John had bought me, and I handed it to him to hold in safekeeping until I came out of the O.R.

John, my parents, Elaine, Judi, and Rachel were all there to keep me company and wish me well. We all tried to seem cheery and light. The human spirit is amazing. Somehow hope springs eternal even under the bleakest of conditions.

"What's that?" I asked Rachel, noticing a box she was clutching.

"Belgian chocolates. I figured we needed some rich chocolate. When you get out of surgery, you'll have some," she said.

"Not if we eat them all first," my dad said as he opened the lid.

"She can't eat this stuff right after surgery," my mom added, while grabbing a peanut cluster.

"I love your boots," Judi said, referencing the blue paper hospital booties on my feet.

"Manolo Blahnik, darling, they're the very latest from Paris," I responded.

They were all there, my closest friends and family, eating, laughing, and trying to be cheerful in an effort to conceal their concerns. When the doctors arrived, everyone but John, my designated partner, was asked to leave. We all kissed and hugged good-bye. My mom, who kissed the hardest and hugged the longest, had to be guided out by my dad. There were many last looks between us.

They started me on an I.V., which apparently made me drowsy quite soon thereafter, because John recalls my wearing a big dopey grin and assuring him how great everything was going to be. Then the orderlies arrived to wheel me in for surgery. John walked with me until they turned a corner and I got rolled away, leaving him behind. He said I was still smiling as I disappeared around the bend.

That's when he said he broke down for the first time since the whole nightmare had begun. Unable to be anything but strong for my benefit since the diagnosis, he suddenly let it all come out as he wept deeply and uncontrollably against a wall. Though not usually given to public displays of emotion, at that moment he couldn't hold back. His release was so full of grief and despair that a kind stranger came over to ask if he was all right and offered to lend a consoling hand.

According to John, for the next few hours while I underwent surgery, my support group of family and friends all clung to each other up in my room. John remained quiet and kept to himself, but the rest responded as Jews do, telling stories and eating comfort food. When my surgeon finally entered, still in her greens, she announced that the operation had gone very well and that she was extremely optimistic. Everyone simultaneously burst into tears, embracing each other and blessing the doctor.

When I awakened in post-op, John was there by my side. It's so weird, being under anesthesia and then coming out of it. It's like waking up from the dead. I had no awareness of what had just happened to me. I didn't feel, dream, or think. Just nothing at all for hours, and now I'd returned. I was back and people were asking me questions and familiar faces were at my bedside telling me things went well. Doctors stood in clumps at the foot of my bed and everyone seemed to have a lot of energy and spoke loudly in an overly cheerful manner. I felt as though I could only stay awake for a minute or two before dozing off again. I was very, very sleepy.

An Asian man was asking me if I was in any pain. *Pain?* I didn't even know what world I was in. Was the surgery over? I had no idea how much time had passed, or really what I was feeling. "I'm trying to determine how much morphine you should get," he said. "I don't want you to be in any pain."

"Well, I don't want to be in any pain, either," I said, "so gimme enough." He then set up a self-medicating gizmo that had a button to push at the end of my I.V. so I could administer the morphine to myself as needed. *Now we're talking.* Gimme a button I can control and I'm happy. I remembered when I had the breast surgery many years earlier. The level of pain I felt as the Novocain began to wear off had been really intense. Man, did that smart. And that was from a cut into the flesh—nothing as major as what I'd just experienced.

They moved me to my room on a gurney. I was one of those sick people with an I.V. bag being pushed through the hospital hallways and elevators. Everyone was there to receive me. My folks and my friends. They seemed really happy to see me. I'm sure the stress of waiting was unbearable.

I noticed a huge round patch stuck to my right breast. When

my surgeon arrived to check on me I questioned her about the patch. I found myself constantly questioning the efficiency of others, but this was my life we were talking about, and I felt like I had a right, ya know what I mean? Anyway, I'm a producer and I can't help it.

Doctor #9 took a look at the patch and explained that it was an estrogen patch to prevent me from going into what's called surgical menopause. In that instant, I thought about the radical effect on my body of suddenly yanking out every major female-hormone-producing organ. In fact, that's what having a complete hysterectomy amounted to.

But, for some reason—and maybe this had been explained to me at an earlier examination—I remembered that hormone patches should be placed on fatty tissue between the waist and the thigh, but never the breast. *Now they're going to give me breast cancer, too!* I thought. Doctor #9 casually explained that the post-op nurse must have mistakenly placed the patch there because that's where they often put the nitroglycerin patch on heart patients. That's nice, but I didn't have heart surgery, I had a hysterectomy, and I started ripping at the patch on my tit. Doctor #9 said not to remove it until she sent for a nurse to bring up a new one and put it in the proper place.

"And will you mention to the post-op nurse what she did wrong and to be more careful next time?" I suggested. She said she would.

When I asked her why something on my right side seemed to be hurting more than my left, she told me the pain I was feeling might be due to the appendectomy. *"WHAT APPENDECTOMY?"* I exclaimed.

"You were at risk of it getting infected and we don't want to have to cut into your abdomen again," she responded. But why didn't we discuss all this before? Shouldn't I have known that standard procedure called for my appendix to be removed along with the hysterectomy? Even though her reasons made sense, the bottom line was, she forgot to mention it. It may not have been a big deal to her, but this was *my* body, *my* reproductive organs, and *my* appendix. It was a big deal to me.

I think back to the anger and resentment I felt toward everyone for letting my condition go undiagnosed for so long. At the time I needed someone to blame to make sense of it all. What a high price I paid for other people's negligence. I felt so victimized. But Doctor #9 delicately suggested I try to move on, that in so doing I'd help my own recovery. John agreed and said, "You've got to remain positive. Pointing fingers is not going to get you well." It wasn't easy, though. I was darkly embittered as I lay in my hospital bed brooding over the pickle I was in.

By early evening, after everyone had left, and it was just me and John, it became clear that I wasn't breathing right. I complained to the nurse, who called for the doctor—not my surgeon but someone who worked under her. When he arrived, John and I were both concerned as we watched him check how many breaths I took per minute. It was about six, when it should have been at least twenty. I don't know why I wasn't breathing more. I just was too tired and kept nodding off into such a deep sleep I'd stop breathing for a while. As it turned out, the problem was that I'd received too much morphine. All afternoon I was pushing my I.V. button, and no one realized they'd set each dose too high for me. That's nice, so now what do we do?

"Is there a shot I could get to counter it?" I asked the doctor. But he shook his head no and muttered something about it just needing to wear off. Then he looked up at John and suggested he keep an eye on my breathing for the next couple of hours. So dear sweet John pulled up a chair right alongside my bed and watched me very closely.

A million things can go wrong. I saw that movie *Hospital*.

I knew about Dana Carvey's going in for heart surgery and his surgeon's operating on the wrong artery. Even Howie, when going in for knee surgery, had the foresight to tape a sign to his good knee that read NOT THIS ONE. So after about twenty minutes, when John's eyes were beginning to close, I forced myself to stay awake just long enough to say, "Get me round-the-clock private nurses before they kill me."

My Week in the Hospital

June 22–June 25, 2000

enid and Harriet were my private nurses for the five days I was in the hospital. I've never been one to throw money away; I have far too much respect for the struggle it takes to earn it. But under the circumstances, I thought it a worthwhile expense. After everything I'd been through, I'm afraid I wasn't very trusting of the medical community.

Enid was the night nurse. She was the first shift to arrive, an older woman with an eastern European accent. She was heavyset, but pretty, too, and seemed very uncomfortable as she passed the night hours sitting in the hard chair next to my bed reading her book and tending to me. The hospital brought a cot into my room for John to sleep on, and that was where he slept for the duration of my stay. Side by side we were, his cot next to my bed and Enid's chair next to me—an odd trio at best. It was all for one and one for all. Enid talked about her daughter, her deceased husband, and the old country. She had a grandmotherly quality to her that was comforting. John watched TV and read mostly. I was never alone, I was never neglected.

The first night sucked. I was up, I was asleep, I was in pain, I was cranky, I was crying, I was a real prize. The floor nurses were in throughout the night to check stuff and none of us felt good in the morning. John called my folks to tell them to come later, but even later wasn't late enough. I really wasn't up for anyone, not even my folks. This was partly due to my need to be "on" for them. I should have just let it all hang out like I seemed to be able to do with John and not concern myself with worrying about their worrying.

Regardless, when they were due to arrive, I hurriedly applied some blush and under-eye concealer to try to look like I hadn't just had a radical hysterectomy and appendectomy as well as been up all night. Moments after the last brushstroke of blush I suddenly felt so sick to my stomach I thought I was going to vomit, and frantically urged John to give me a pail. I'd been told that as anesthesia wears off you can get very nauseous, but until that moment I'd not experienced it. Nothing much came up, since I hadn't eaten anything solid in days. My body was revolting against my futile attempts to camouflage my cancer surgery. What a yutz!

My parents arrived at one of my lowest points. I couldn't fake that I was well, and I couldn't cope with them seeing I wasn't. I don't know how to explain it, but I needed to just be able to relax about looking and feeling miserable. But after a lifetime of trying never to give my parents any reason to worry, I was unable to let them witness that. At my request, that was their last visit to the hospital. I don't know how John told them, but I dumped that responsibility onto him. I'm sure this was strange for all of them. John wasn't Peter, someone my parents had known for more than twenty years—he was someone they'd only met a few times before. Maybe that made it easier for him, but not for them. I just wanted to be left alone. I didn't want company. I didn't have the strength to battle my issues with my parents. People don't change overnight; at least I couldn't.

So many things can go wrong after surgery. I never realized

how critical the first few days of post-op truly are. Enid would repeatedly ask me to blow into a device that's designed to help get the lungs working fully in an attempt to prevent pneumonia from developing. "Blow harder and make the balls rise," she'd command. "That's my specialty, honey, step aside," I quipped.

A nurse came in with these leg massagers that wrapped around my legs like pants and pulsated up and down to stimulate my circulation.

"What are these for?" I asked the nurse.

"Prevents blood clots, common after abdominal surgery," she explained, while strapping them on my legs.

"Blood clots? Oy," I mumbled, as I looked down on the two huge blue vinyl blowup sleeves contracting and expanding around each leg. "Oh, this feels kinda nice, actually. Ahhh," I sighed, as I began to relax and get into it. A few hours later, I pushed the intercom next to my bed. "Do you think I could get those leg things again?" A few hours later, "Excuse me, but I'd love those leg things again, please." Finally the nurse entered my room with my very own pair.

"Here," she said, dropping them in my lap. "Just keep 'em." Was it something I said? . . .

I never used a bedpan; they discouraged it. So several hours after my surgery I was trying to swing each leg off the bed and, along with my morphine I.V., slowly shuffle over to the bathroom.

John and Enid were always by my side helping me get around. It took the greatest of efforts to make the smallest of moves. The hospital staff was pleasantly surprised that I was able to urinate as soon as I did, and of course being the overachiever I am, I took pride in my superior recuperative powers. That was a wrong road of thinking I ventured down, and something that gave me nothing but grief. It was stupid of me to try to be the best patient. I wasn't in competition with anyone. I should have been smart enough to let my poor broken body get the absolute rest it needed. I think psychologically I wanted so badly to put it all behind me and just be normal again. Never having had major surgery before, I didn't realize that the surgery isn't the end of anything. It marks the beginning of a long and arduous period of healing and recovery.

Apparently, one of the most important functions that needs to kick in and put you on the road to recovery is finally moving your bowels. And that brings us to Harriet, my day nurse, who made it her personal quest to get me to take a shit.

Harriet seemed like a middle-aged valley girl. Simple and uncomplicated, with a passion for administering enemas. Now, I don't know about you, but I'd never experienced one of those before. There I was on my knees, getting what she referred to as a "Harris Flush"—in the presence of my boyfriend, no less. And after many failed attempts, John actually jumped for joy, cheering me on, when we finally hit pay dirt. *Eureka!* It was at this point, if it hadn't already happened, that all mystery was lost between us. Not that that's a bad thing, mind you. You make trade-offs in life, and mine was mystery in exchange for the deep and loving bond that only extreme flatulence can bring.

Surprisingly, this small triumph for Harriet seemed to make Enid jealous, because an odd hostility began between the two. The Day Nurse versus the Night Nurse! All we needed was a mud pit, a referee, and a couple of string bikinis. I couldn't believe that, of all the possible combinations of people the agency could have sent over, I ended up with two women who hated each other.

Enid was more overt in her disdain, and shared with us her story of just where all the animosity began. It had to do with money and shifts and Harriet inadvertently saying something that made Enid look bad. Enid made sure we understood that she didn't think Harriet was mean, or a bad nurse, just stupid. Oh fine, that's nice to know.

It was rather entertaining for John and I to watch the catfight unfold between them. I remember during one change in shift Enid was helping me back to my bed from the bathroom when Harriet arrived. As Enid held one elbow and Harriet grabbed the other, the two of them fought across me.

"You're late," Enid scolded.

Harriet, waving a small brown paper bag, said, "I'm not late, I had to pick up her acidophilus." She was supplementing the hospital medical supplies with her own homeopathy, but Enid just couldn't stand her and the two of them began pulling on each arm, fighting over who'd get to put me to bed.

Finally, I stood my ground and shouted, "*Enough!* I can't stand the fighting."

"Who's fighting? We're not fighting," they both said, like little kids who're caught red-handed but deny fault anyway.

"Enid, you were great last night and I thank you, so go get some rest and let Harriet take over," I said diplomatically. Exasperated, Enid acquiesced, mumbling the words "she's so stupid" under her breath as she packed her bag.

In truth, they each had very different responsibilities. The nights were always more difficult for me. The pain would be worse, my temperature would go up, and I'd get more emotional. But Enid was like a rock, comforting, consoling, and caring.

During Harriet's shift it was an entirely different situation. Harriet needed to get things accomplished. During the day I needed to walk, I needed to shit, and I needed to eat.

And like a bad sitcom, Enid and Harriet continued to bicker at each changing of the guard both morning and evening. John and I called them "Heckle and Jeckle." But after three nights of sleeping on a cot, John had had just about enough of them. By day four, we'd walk the halls on our own, letting Harriet take breaks or run errands, and Enid would sit outside the room at night reading, and would be called in only if needed. I didn't have the heart to dismiss them early, and who knew? A complication could've set in, no matter how good my progress . . . better safe than sorry.

Walking down the hallways on my floor was a trip unto itself. I'd always seen those sickly-looking people in hospital gowns shuffling down the halls, pushing their I.V.'s, and thought how terribly self-conscious I'd feel doing that. But guess what? It's not so embarrassing when it's you. For some reason, all the stuff that concerned me when I was a well visitor flew out the window when I was a recovering patient. John said half the time my ass was hanging out of my gown. I was wondering what that draft was . . .

I *really* appreciated all the art that lined the hospital's hallway walls. I studied each piece as if I were in a gallery or a museum. It didn't matter whether it was a poster, litho, or original, each work filled me with its beauty. I was lucky that Cedars understands the importance of aesthetics; it truly did make a difference.

Sometimes there'd be a man walking down the halls in his hospital gown, pushing his I.V. I remember one time I decided to try to catch up to and beat him in a race he knew nothing about, all the while covering the event like it was a horse race. "And here comes Fran, the long shot of the day, closing in on the favorite. And there's Fran running neck and neck, and now she takes the lead! And it's Fran by a length!" The man had no clue, but I for some reason got a real kick out of it. That was the first time since my surgery I started to feel a little joy, as if my old personality was coming back. John and I explored all the closed doors on my floor. We entered offices and rooms like a couple of mischievous kids.

I hated that I couldn't get fresh air. All of the windows were screwed shut. How are you supposed to get better when you're surrounded by sick people and can't even open a window? I'm a big believer in the curative powers of fresh air and a nice breeze. Whenever anyone has a cold, I immediately open a window to get everything circulating. Perhaps I'm trusting in old wives' tales, but I put great stock in fresh bed linens, clean pajamas, opened windows, and chicken soup.

When Rachel and Greg were preparing to stop by for a visit they phoned to ask if I needed anything. I simply replied, "A Phillips-head screwdriver." Greg, bless his heart, was so happy to help he picked one up at a hardware store on their way to the hospital.

It was great watching Greg and John roll up their sleeves and get to work. What is it about men and tools? It was just what John needed after spending the last few days in that hospital with nothing to do but read and watch TV. In no time the windows in my room were wide open and beautiful summer breezes were blowing through the curtains. I was worried we'd get in trouble for doing it, but everyone turned a blind eye.

It wasn't long before my doctors switched me from morphine to lesser painkillers. But some upset my stomach or made me drowsy, while others made me nervous or put me in a bad mood. There's a million different prescriptions out there. I forced the physician to discuss all options until I felt the best I could under the circumstances. I started taking Vicodin, which is a fairly strong narcotic but really effective against pain. In fact, I'd say it works almost too well, because during the pill's peak performance, I felt so good I ended up bending, lifting, and doing more than I should have. Some people take Vicodin to get high, but it didn't give *me* a buzz. Damn! Also, it would aggravate my stomach if I didn't take it with food. So during the night I was forcing myself to eat crackers and pudding and rice hoarded from the day. Okay, I'll admit it, at first I relished the excuse to eat starchy stuff like macaroni and cheese, but after a while even I had had enough!

It was gross, pushing food down when I didn't want it, so I

asked what else I could take. I decided to try a new drug called Vioxx that's described as being a twenty-four-hour, Advil-type medicine. I liked this pill. It was easy to take—only one a day and it seemed to do the trick. The hitch was that it lasted for only sixteen or eighteen hours out of the twenty-four. So I mostly stayed with the Vioxx for the sixteen hours I was awake, then at night would knock myself out with a Vicodin. It was just a matter of trial and error before I figured out which routine worked best.

Nobody ever knocked when they entered, and one nurse after another kept walking into my room. It took getting used to, not having locks on the doors and people coming and going at will. I soon realized that the only thing private about a private room is that you aren't sharing it with other sick people. That's where the privacy begins and ends.

On the third day of my hospital stay, my surgeon came waltzing into my room, all chipper and smiles, followed by Doctor #8, the gynecologist who'd finally diagnosed me. I was still mad at all the doctors I'd seen, but her above all. This was the doctor who'd initially insisted I didn't have cancer and had given me birth control pills with estrogen! I began bleeding 24/7, which I found very alarming. She, who was supposed to be the big Hoo-Ha, with all her books and TV appearances—shouldn't she have tested me sooner?

My surgeon knew I was angry at my gynecologist, yet she let Doctor #8 come right in with her. Why hadn't she told the gynecologist to wait outside while she inquired if I wanted company? I suppose I should have expected it: Doctors align with doctors, and the surgeon wasn't about to get in the middle of it. There was the gynecologist, acting like she was the heroine of my story, glowing with pride. Had she forgotten the other details along the way? Well, I hadn't been in therapy for as long as I had to remain passive. No sir. I'd spent too many nights agonizing over my fate not to open a mouth!

There she sat. There they both sat, and I was going to get some satisfaction. I was sick of wondering why. I had cancer, and I'd had half my guts removed, and I simply didn't give a damn who'd feel uncomfortable by my confrontation.

So I just came right out and said it. "Ya know, I have to ask you, why didn't you give me the D&C right away?" With that, the smile on the gynecologist's face disappeared.

"Well, I wanted to go the less invasive route first. It was only for a month," she responded, seemingly surprised I was even barking up this tree.

"Less invasive? It's a two-minute test." I was becoming incensed. A two-minute test that could have diagnosed my cancer two years ago, if any of my doctors had thought to give me one. Meanwhile, it wasn't a month I was on the pill, it was a week. What made her think I, in my right mind, would *ever* have stayed on those pills for a whole month when they were making me bleed 24/7?

And that was when I really put up my dukes. "I mean, you weren't the first doctor I'd gone to. You *knew* how long I'd had these symptoms. And Doctor #9 said that everyone is taught in medical school, when there's bleeding between periods, you biopsy." What did I care if I was pitting one against the other. That *is* what she said. Who was I protecting?

"Fran, don't forget, it was Doctor #8 who did diagnose you," the surgeon cut in.

"I understand that, and I'm grateful for it," I acknowledged, because who's kidding who, I was glad that *someone* had finally figured out what the hell was wrong with me.

That's when Doctor #8 surprised me with her response: "Fran, if it makes you feel any better, I've given this a great deal of thought. In the future, when patients have symptoms such as yours, I'll be more apt to perform a D&C to rule out uterine cancer *before* prescribing hormone replacement."

That's all I needed to hear. "Well, I appreciate your saying that. It does make me feel better." And that was that. They left through the unlocked door of my hospital room. Probably couldn't wait to get out of there fast enough. I felt vindicated, though. The question of *why* that had consumed me was satisfied and could finally be put to rest. More or less . . .

The next day, unbeknownst to me, a beautiful vase filled with two dozen roses arrived addressed to Fran Drescher. They were from one of the executive producers on *The Nanny*. It was lovely, generous, and thoughtful of the sender, but to John it signaled that the cat was out of the bag! News of my cancer must have hit the airwaves.

John didn't allow the flowers to be brought into the room. Instead, he kept them at the nurses' station until he could figure out what was happening. Obviously, there'd been a breach in security, and the last thing he wanted was my getting upset. When a nurse from the floor said there was a call at the desk, he nonchalantly left to answer it. Allan, Elaine's husband, had just taken a call for Elaine, who already was on her way to the hospital. It was from a newspaper asking questions about my cancer. John took down the information and waited anxiously for Elaine's arrival.

Even though all this was happening around me, I had no clue, and John was determined to keep it that way. When Elaine arrived with not one, but two fishbowls of white flowers, John pushed her back into the hallway before I even knew what was going on. Slightly annoyed, picking freesias off her chest, Elaine listened to John explain the situation's urgency. Tearfully, he said, "You're going to have to be the one to tell her. I don't have the heart."

Elaine immediately shifted into full-throttle mode. There wasn't a moment to lose, and with New York's being three hours ahead, she had to jump on this pronto or who knew how the headlines might read? So she contacted Cari, the publicist I'd worked with throughout the years on *The Nanny,* and asked her to return the reporter's call and do a press release. Meanwhile, I was inside my room trying to down some turkey tetrazzini that I'd ordered from the menu, without even a hint of suspicion. Got any butter?

It was on the day I was scheduled to be released, five days after my surgery, that they told me. Elaine arrived as John and I were finishing breakfast at the little dining table in my room. By this point I was trying to shift into somewhat normal behavior, like eating at a table and walking unassisted to the bathroom. John braced himself for how I'd react when Elaine told me. He knew that was why she was there. He was counting on my usual reaction. I'd get very upset but then, in almost a childlike way, having had my release, quickly feel better.

Now, Elaine has never been one to pussyfoot around. "A good surgeon makes his amputation with one clean cut. A bad one hacks away with multiple cuts and leaves a lot of scars in the process." That's what she always said, and they're words she lives by, too. So without any mollycoddling she simply told me, "Fran, a New York paper picked up on your cancer and wrote an article about it."

As anticipated, I immediately burst into tears, dropping my face into my hands. This meant I couldn't sweep this illness under the rug, quietly recover, put everything back to normal and deny my cancer, even to myself. Essentially, I'd been "outed." The illness was official now. I was a cancer victim and the world knew it. Elaine pulled a fax copy from her purse. "I brought it so you can read it and see it wasn't bad. They kept it simple." The headline read MISS FINE IS FINE. She was right, it wasn't bad or sensational. But still, I felt exposed. And, as John had anticipated, I let out all the pent-up emotions and fears and then was done with it.

It was Sunday, in the late morning, when I returned home. John and I drove in one car and Elaine followed with the flowers in the other. My parents anxiously awaited our arrival. When we walked in the house it was so white and clean and filled with fresh flowers. I was so happy to see the smiling, loving faces of my parents and feel the kisses and licks from my beloved Chester.

John and I walked out onto the deck of my house that overlooks the sea. If ever I had a religious experience, this was it; all the celestial beings in heaven seemed to gather around to welcome us home. Words couldn't even begin to do justice to the miracle of it all. The breezes were blustery but warm, the clouds were puffy and white, moving across a sky as blue as a Maxfield Parrish painting, and the ocean itself seemed to dance in soft white peaks as it sailed across the horizon.

The aliveness of it all; the love of my parents and Elaine and Chester; the deep, deep feelings of love and devotion from John— all combined to give me the feeling that somehow, despite everything, my life was going to be okay.

First Week Home

June 25–July 2, 2000

P eople always wonder whether they should call someone who's ill or recovering or grieving. I, too, would hesitate at times, concerned I might be bothersome. Human beings are often awkward and uncomfortable around others' pain. But I can now say for sure that it's nice to be on the receiving end of people's thoughtfulness. I didn't always feel up to taking a call from a well-wisher, but I always got the message and appreciated the show of concern.

When someone you know is in a bad way, make that call, pay a visit, send some flowers. I was thrilled when friends and relatives sent bouquets, balloons, teddy bears, sweets, pajamas, bath products, and books, mostly self-help books. I had all the time in the world to read, but I just felt too lousy to concentrate. Not until I felt better did I even crack the first one.

So the books stacked up on a shelf as I watched endless hours of the Food Network. Who needed some know-it-all self-help author giving pep talks on how to be positive? To take my mind off things, I needed overweight people in orange kitchens playing with food. Molto Mario, Emeril, and Two Fat Ladies became my roly-poly bedside companions. It was the perfect distraction. Not heady, thirty minutes, and all about food. It just put me into such a relaxed place; the equivalent of sucking my thumb and twirling my hair as a kid.

I also spent time surfing the net, browsing rental properties in Tuscany. This pastime transported me to beautiful worlds far from my recovery bed. I'd dream of the day when I'd be able to rent a place in Italia and stay for a month or two. Each time I found a place I loved, I'd print the listing and stack it with the others on my wish list.

My right arm Kathryn would send me haiku e-mails and profound words from great philosophers. She'd share her own brave struggles with illness and surgery, quoting Hindu and Buddhist passages. She tirelessly helped keep my life running smoothly when I was too weak to pick up a pencil, let alone answer a call. She kept things afloat. She was a lifesaver.

My folks, who were sleeping in the guest house, arrived every day to cook breakfast and didn't leave until after the last dinner dish was cleared. Dad would sit on the deck and read his novels while Mom waited on me hand and foot. John, who literally moved in the day I learned I had cancer, never left my side. I wanted to resume writing the MTV pilot that had been derailed by my illness.

Camelia, my friend and coworker who's very robust in her hearty affection, had a take-charge attitude. "I'm here for you, girl," she'd always say. She organized all the thank-yous for the gifts I'd received from well-wishers, so I never stressed out over any of it. She talked about the loss of her first husband, told me of a girlfriend who'd survived cancer, and shared stories about her two lovely daughters.

Then there were the visitors. Some of my girlfriends stopped by one afternoon. Each brought a little gift and stayed for a few hours. The girls wanted to hear the whole story: What were my symptoms, who were the doctors, when did it all begin? With respect to the procedures I'd undergone, everyone agreed that never getting your period or going through menopause was the definite upside.

They all wanted to see my incision, which I freely showed them. But upon exposing myself, I felt like a freak. Different from the rest. The unlucky one. What were they thinking? Probably they were glad it wasn't them. Of all the girls in this group, I think I was the last person anyone expected to get cancer. They all had experienced gynecological problems ranging from precancerous cells (determined by Pap tests) to cysts (found by ultrasound) to endometriosis (scar tissue that grows abnormally). Not me, though. We all sat on my sickbed chewing the fat like everything was normal. How ironic that I was always the one who'd never showed weakness in this area.

My girlfriends all played significant roles in my recovery. Shortly before my diagnosis, I'd had an urge to see my old friend Michelle, whom I hadn't seen in years. This was one of those instincts that, in retrospect, made me think I was being nudged by the angels, because Michelle was the only one, in the end, who wasn't working and completely available to me during those early weeks after my surgery.

She reminds me of my mom in her warm, loving, and nurturing ways. I remember when she, my mom, and I took one of our first walks together. I had to move very slowly, and I couldn't go far, but we noticed a house for sale that was open for viewing. We went inside and had some fun exploring. The house wasn't far down the road, but far enough for me. Afterward, we turned around and slowly walked back to the car. I couldn't wait to go home and lie down.

I can remember vividly when Donna called from New York to say that Danny was coming to town. We were very excited to see him. He was in L.A. for the filming of *Pearl Harbor*. It was only my first week home after the surgery, and by his reaction when he first laid eyes on me, I think he was expecting me to look like I was at death's door. He seemed so relieved and happy.

I didn't want to look like someone with cancer, so I spent a lot of time vacillating about what I was going to wear. I just didn't want to feel insecure about how others perceived me. I gotta admit, that day Danny stopped by I did manage to pull it together in a soft jersey miniskirt and sleeveless tee. He just couldn't get over me and I beamed with pride.

I was inspired to prepare a good lunch for him since he's always such a generous host himself. As I was putting together the main course (shrimp marinara over pasta, with salad), my mother took the spaghetti pot out of my hands and scolded me for overdoing it. I insisted I felt fine, but it was really the painkillers talking. If drugs like that weren't available, I'm sure I would have been totally bedridden and miserable. When Danny was there we ate and drank like old times, but when he left I needed to lie down.

Whenever I had visitors I'd crack open a bottle of wine and put out a spread. I don't know, perhaps it made me feel more like a hostess than a cancer patient. What none of the doctors had mentioned to me was that it's not really a good idea to drink alcohol when recovering from surgery, because it slows the healing process. As it was, I'd adopted an "I don't give a fuck" attitude, feeling I was owed some self-indulgence after everything I'd been through.

The ultimate example of this was the first time I got a craving for KFC fried chicken fingers and sent Ramon out to get me a bucket pronto. "Hurry, Ramon. Put the mop down and get to that Colonel now," I said with a crazed look in my eye.

"But I heard those chickens have no beaks," he said.

"I don't care, Ramon, *go!*" I insisted, grabbing the mop from his hand. From that point forward I scarfed down one bucket after another for months, until one day it became all about the Taco Bell Chalupa. Ten pounds later, I'm still paying.

I think in that first week home, I was still in a state of shock over what had happened. Distracted by all the well-wishers and numbed by the painkillers, I didn't allow reality to set in. By the second week, however, as things settled down, that all changed.

Fourth of July, 2000

It had been a little over a week since my release from the hospital and I wasn't happy. The only times I seemed happy were when I was trying to be the superwoman I'm not. I acted like everything was okay, seeking praise for how well I looked or how fast I recovered. I call it "doin' the seal act," because that's what it often feels like. I've always needed to appear strong and together. In my entire life I can barely remember a moment when I allowed myself to really break down and cry in front of others. I'd always heard people say, "If you keep everything bottled up, you're gonna give yourself a cancer." Maybe there's some truth in that.

"Fran never cried," my mom always said when describing my childhood. I don't really think that's healthy, but growing up in my house it seemed praiseworthy to me. Even after I'd been raped at gunpoint, Elaine sat with me on Donna's porch and felt the need to say, "It's okay to cry." But all I could do was hold back the tears, unable to speak in full sentences for fear the pain would come pouring out like water from a broken dam. Couldn't let that happen. Uh-uh. No sir, not me.

I hated the way my body looked after the surgery. I thought it would never return to its previous state. So swollen and bruised, it didn't even look like my shape. I worried I'd be stuck forever with this matronly, misshapen, ugly, bruised body. I didn't want John to see what I looked like. But *I* saw—as I stared in my completely mirrored bathroom, lit by a skylight, no less. My flesh was shades of green and purple in spots. Every ripple, every bulge, everything looked worse in those mirrors under the cold, harsh shaft of light from above.

And the incision! Oh my God. *I'm ruined,* I thought. Such a cruel-looking red horizontal gash across my pubic line. They'd shaved my hair for the surgery so the scar was shockingly noticeable. And then there was the estrogen patch. To add insult to injury, I had to look at this plastic patch stuck to my hip. Stuck there for the rest of my life. Stuck to my body like I was stuck in my situation.

Finally, I just gave up on myself. There was nothing I could do but put on some clothes and walk away from the mirrors. I slid back into bed where John lay reading. It was hard to find a position that was comfortable. My insides felt gelatinous, and every move I made seemed to discombobulate already traumatized organs—ones that hadn't yet rerooted themselves in my newly hollowed-out abdomen.

I laid on my back staring up at the ceiling and began to feel sorry for John. As tears rolled out the corners of my eyes, I worried my relationship with him was too new to garner this kind of loyalty and devotion. I decided he was responding out of guilt and obligation. I knew those feelings ruled him—*imprisoned* is a better word—and I never wanted him to feel that being with me was "doing time."

When he asked me what the matter was as I wept by his side, the words that came out didn't acknowledge my concern for *his* burden. Rather it was *my* pain, *my* profound sorrow, *my* grief that erupted.

I didn't just cry, I bellowed. Clenching my hands into fists, I pulled on his T-shirt and buried my face in his chest. He could barely understand what I was saying as I let out what could only be described as a primal scream. There was so much raw emotion, I can't even begin to imagine what it was like to be on the receiving end. He tried to calm me, to quiet me, but like a hysterical child, I eventually just wore myself out. As I lay on his chest, limp with exhaustion, the two of us retreated quietly into ourselves.

Once again, I began worrying about John. Tending to my needs both day and night was all-consuming. The pain and grief were overwhelming, and it was beginning to sap him of his strength. Being the main caregiver in a situation like this can be like trying to save a drowning person whose panicked efforts to save himself almost pull you *both* under.

I also worried that John wasn't opening up to his friends, sharing the nightmare with them. None seemed to have an awareness of what we were really going through. Once I heard him on the phone saying, "Everyone's fine, things are great," and I questioned why he said that. No one was fine, nothing was great, and his friends should have been told so they could start functioning like true friends. But John never feels comfortable complaining about his needs. I could appreciate his not wanting to burden me, but he certainly should have opened up to them.

When one of them was having a Fourth of July party in the afternoon, I encouraged John to go. My parents would be with me. The one thing I asked is that he tell his friends the truth, that we were in hell over here: "Life is shit. Fran is in pain and cries all night. I'm in over my head. Please come up to the house and visit us. I need my friends to support me." Through it all, I knew how much better I felt soliciting the help of my friends, and I wanted him to do the same.

He was afraid he'd be a downer at the party if he dumped his problems on his friends who wanted to have a fun afternoon. "That's what friends are for!" I insisted. So halfheartedly, he left my side for just a few hours—literally, for the first time in weeks—to go to the Fourth of July party.

Unfortunately, once he left to go do his own thing, I couldn't keep up my facade anymore. My parents came over to stay with me, and they both sat on my deck reading their books while I began to feel like a chipped soup bowl from the reject china shop. Everyone was out having fun, going to parties, and eating barbecue—everyone but me, that is. John was healthy and young. All the people having fun at the party were healthy and young. But I wasn't healthy *or* young.

The cheese stands alone. That was me. The house was too quiet and the isolation seemed to point up the terrible turn my life had taken. Even my parents, who sat side by side reading, could claim a deeply committed, mutually loving, long-term relationship *and* great health. In my frustration I walked out on the deck, looking to instigate something. "We should have made plans today," I said petulantly.

"You need to rest," my dad said.

"But everyone's having fun and I want to have fun, too," I insisted. My poor parents.

"You just had major surgery, how can you go to a party?" my mom reasoned, but I began to cry. I stood in my pajamas on a hot Fourth of July afternoon acting like the kid I never allowed myself to be.

"Well, we should have invited a few friends here to make it seem festive instead of depressing and sad," I whined. I'm sure I never would have entered such a funk had John stayed with me that afternoon. But when he left, it crystallized who was the ill one and who was well. It was a bitter pill to swallow. My mom desperately tried to make amends by suggesting we invite people over, but it really wasn't about that. The loss I was feeling couldn't be filled by calling a few friends. I wanted my life back.

John was gone only a few short hours. It was good for him to get out, see his friends, be around people. Upon his return he shared a vivid account of his afternoon: who was at the party, what food was served, and what was said. He's a good storyteller and I hung on every word.

That night a few friends stopped by on their way home from wherever. We all stood on the edge of my deck overlooking the ocean and the coastline, watching fireworks bursting everywhere in the sky. We'd ordered in Chinese food for dinner, but my parents left shortly before it began. I called them, so excited, to tell them how special it all was. My mom was so relieved to hear me sounding so much better than before, she wept. But that's how it went at that time. Sometimes it was like I'd smacked into a brick wall; other times I was cheerfully distracted.

The next morning, though, I hit a new all-time low. There was no turning back. I was a woman who'd never be able to have a baby. I looked over at John and began to feel anger. If only he hadn't dragged his heels about freezing an embryo, I wouldn't be in this mess. In my need to point blame, he became my next victim. "If only I'd frozen an embryo when I wanted to. If only I'd followed my instincts, if only *you* . . ." I never finished my thought because he angrily retaliated.

"Shut up!" he screamed with a venomous look in his eye. He began to cry as he said, "How dare you, how dare you blame me for anything? Do you know what it's been like for me, what I've gone through?"

I felt terrible. I'd indulged my self-pity and in the process hurt John deeply. He got out of bed. He couldn't look at me anymore. I'd gone too far. It pained me to see how much I'd hurt him. Well, what could I do but apologize, beg his forgiveness, and hope he could somehow understand that I carried a lot of anger about what had happened to me?

The truth was, I wasn't even thinking straight. It wouldn't have mattered *when* he agreed to make an embryo because the cold, hard reality of the situation was that I'd already had the cancer. The outcome was a foregone conclusion. I had to learn to manage my anger and never again turn on my loved ones. This was my fate and that was that.

The next afternoon my cousin Susan from Las Vegas flew down to visit for the day. Having company was always a nice distraction, so I looked forward to her arrival. I knew I wasn't acting like myself, but hoped a visitor could help pull me out of the rut I was in. Who *was* I? Not the Fran who'd triumphed over hard times and countless obstacles her whole life.

"Should we do chicken and spaghetti?" Mom asked, while standing in the doorway of my room with a dish towel tucked in her waist. I slowly began swinging my legs off the bed to come and help her in the kitchen. "Don't get up, I'll make it," she insisted.

"No, I wanna help," I said, pushing my body into a standing position.

"All right. Well, if you sit by the counter and tell me what to make, I'll make it. Ya need help walking?"

What was I, an invalid? "No, I'm okay. Let's make a big salad with the chicken," I said, pulling myself up the step from my sunken bedroom.

In two minutes my mom was all over the kitchen, opening cabinets and pulling stuff out of the fridge. In comparison to me, she seemed so bouncy and spry. I was like an old lady and she was like a young girl. Dad helped by setting the table.

"Do we want big forks *and* little forks?" he asked, holding up two fistfuls of utensils.

"Yes," I answered, "and also knives for the chicken and spoons for twirling the pasta," I added.

"Why waste?" Dad said. "All I need is one fork. I don't need a knife, I don't need a spoon." There's that Depression-baby mentality kicking in again.

"Why don't we eat with our feet and not use anything?" I said sarcastically.

My mom threw me a glance. "What are you answering him for? It's a sickness with you, Morty. *Now go set the table!*" she scolded, while emptying a box of Ronzoni into a pot of hot water.

My dad walked past me, holding all the flatware. "Now you got me in trouble," he muttered under his breath, then threw me a knowing wink.

"When did he become such a pain in the ass?" Mom asked rhetorically, popping the chicken into the oven. But this wasn't anything new; Dad had always been nuts about waste.

When Cousin Susan arrived, we all agreed she looked great dolled up in a straw hat and summer clothes. John poured us some white wine and everyone sat down at the dining-room table. Food was being passed from one hand to another, but Mom made up my plate because she thought the serving bowls were too heavy for me to lift.

As Cousin Susan was telling us about the Las Vegas real estate boom and her pending divorce, John suddenly made a deep, guttural throat-clearing sound. I looked over to him to see if he was choking. "Are you okay?" I asked.

"I'm okay. I thought I was about to choke on a piece of chicken there for a minute, but I'm not," he said. He'd no sooner finished saying he wasn't choking than Cousin Susan began to choke.

"What's with the chicken?" John said, putting down his fork loaded with poultry.

Just then, Susan shot up from her chair, still holding her glass of Pinot Grigio, and began wheezing. She *really* seemed to be choking! I immediately jumped out of my seat and rushed to her aid. "Oh my God, she's choking!" Mom screamed.

"What's goin' on here?" my dad shouted, still chewing a mouthful of food.

Now, I'd witnessed a choking in a restaurant once, and it was the exact same thing. The man stood up, started pacing and gasping for breath. Another patron grabbed him and started doing the Heimlich maneuver while the rest of us sat dumbfounded.

So I knew exactly what to do. I immediately grabbed Cousin Susan from behind and for the first time in my life attempted the Heimlich maneuver.

"Don't rip your stitches," my mom hysterically shouted as I kept thrusting Susan against my stomach. Susan's little straw hat flipped off her head with the first jolt and lay upside down on the floor. Each time I pushed my fist under her rib cage with the palm of my other hand, the wine in her glass splashed across the room. Over and over I repeated the maneuver until finally, miraculously, the lodged meat projectiled out of her mouth and onto the floor. We all went over to inspect the tiny piece of regurgitated chicken.

"It's not even that big," Mom commented.

"Would ya look at that," Dad said in wonderment.

"Sweetie, you responded so quickly," John said in awe.

"I told you, I'm good in an emergency," I reminded.

"Fran, you saved my life," Cousin Susan said, still gasping. I really *did* save her life. Wow. How crazy was that?

Mom grabbed her napkin and picked up the culprit as we all resumed our positions around the table. Cousin Susan once again began chatting about her life, while shoveling food in her mouth. Mom and Dad sat at the edge of their seats watching her every last bite. John, who lost his appetite, pushed his plate away, while I began twirling my pasta, feeling a bit more like my old self.

Sex

Within the first two weeks after my operation, the surgeon called me at home with the pathology reports. "You're completely clean, there was no spread of cancer," she announced.

I cried with relief. "Oh, that's great news," I squealed.

"Three pathologists agree, your cancer was at stage one and grade two," she said. That meant that even though there were cells that varied from grades one through four, the majority of the tumor was dominated by grade two cells. "We recommend no postoperative treatment outside your follow-up exams every three months for the next two years and every six months for three years after that," she added.

"When can I start having sex again?" I asked eagerly. I wanted to feel like a woman again, and be able to satisfy John. I knew my libido was intact because there were days when I found myself watching him get dressed and let me tell you, he was lookin' fine! But honestly, I also think I needed to prove to myself that I wasn't damaged goods. I kept thinking John was young and healthy, he could get a woman who *had* a uterus. And I wanted to know if sex would be the same as before. Contrary to the plethora of Jewish-princess sex jokes, I happen to love sex, orgasms, and passionate, sensuous encounters. So what exactly was the deal now that they'd hollowed me out like a Barbie doll?

"Your vaginal canal is completely intact," she said.

"Yeah, and—" I said, expecting more.

"That's it," she stated the facts plainly.

"That's what?" I questioned, unable to picture it.

"We removed the cervix, and sewed you up at the top." All I could picture were those vinyl blowup sex dolls.

"So will John hit a back wall when he's inside me?" I asked.

"Honestly, Fran, there isn't a dick long enough to reach the top," she answered in her usual forthright manner. But then again she'd never met my sweetie . . .

"Will I get wet? Can I still orgasm?" I said, cutting to the chase. I mean, who's kidding whom? I'm a woman with needs.

"Yes, definitely. You'll have full sexual function," she said.

Full sexual function—I liked the sound of that. "But when?" I asked.

"You can try anytime. It's been long enough."

Well, that was music to my ears, as I began eyeballing my man from across the room.

Poor John; he was so nervous about hurting me or ripping something, frankly I don't know how he even got it up, but he managed. We shut off the TV, turned down the lights, and put on some sexy music. I nearly wept when he began to fondle me and I felt the first flurry of tingles. I wished my pubic hair had grown back faster, but tried to push away insecure thoughts as we kissed and slowly began to make love. Actually, to be precise, we slowly began to get *me* off, *slow* being the operative word here. I couldn't quite find it and I was beginning to get nervous.

"It's not gonna happen, let's just forget it," I said. But John urged me to stay with it.

"Don't worry about a result or me or anything, just relax and enjoy the ride," he coaxed. Well, if he was willing to do the driving, taking the ride was the least I could do, so I took his advice and, wouldn't you know it, all of a sudden my breathing deepened, I began to get wet, and then, wonder of wonders, it happened. I went over the top and hit the big O. Ahhh. How amazing is the body? Not two weeks after having all my reproductive organs removed, I was able to have a truly great orgasm! We kissed, we hugged, and I caressed his body the way I knew he liked.

Oh baby, now I was ready to put the machinery to the ultimate test. And for the first time we would do it without a condom. Wasn't much point to it anymore. We were both totally monogamous, HIV negative, and there wasn't a chance in hell of getting pregnant, so why not just go for it? I think we felt a little naughty, not using any protection, and that just simmered things up a bit. I opted for the missionary position. It seemed easiest, and the least taxing on my incision. Plus, being on my back made my still-swollen abdomen look flatter. Entering me was a little difficult, though. We needed oil, saliva, you name it! But there was penetration and mission accomplished!

The best part of all, I had absolutely no cramping afterward. Literally for the first time in years, I was able to make love and not feel like I needed an Advil to dull the pain. I did have some very light staining, but decided not to tell John. Why spoil it? I knew I was going to see the surgeon for a post-op checkup over the next week, so for the moment I chose to ignore it. Being able to make love was a real milestone for us. We'd found ourselves as a man and a woman again. It felt good. *Very* good, and I felt relieved and above all, satisfied.

After that, I felt like the Bionic Woman: "We can rebuild her, we can make her better. . . ."

Radiation Treatment?

July 9, 2000

the day I went back to Cedars, my outlook left something to be desired. My abdomen hurt a great deal, making me regret I'd rushed into having sex and angry I had to contend with any of this. So there we all were, back in the car, heading into town for my first postsurgery checkup. My parents were in the backseat and John drove. The car ride was so painful. It took two pillows to keep me comfortable: I sat on one, and I placed the other between my seat belt and my abdomen.

"Slow down," I yelped, after every bump.

"I'm going twenty miles an hour, Fran," John answered. "If I go any slower, we'll get in an accident." Then it became a group discussion.

"Maybe you should take off the seat belt," Dad said.

"She can't take off the seat belt, Morty. What if we got into an accident?" my mom reasoned.

"Put the seat back."

"Put your legs out."

"Put the back down."

"Everybody calm down. Nothing helps, so let's change the subject!" I shouted.

Then after a long tense silence: "Where we goin' for lunch? Are we meetin' Elaine?" Mom asked.

"Yes. I invited her and Allan, Rachel, and Greg. We're all gonna meet on the patio at Orso's after my checkup," I said, grateful we were onto something new.

"That's nice, I like that place," Mom added.

"I could eat pasta every day," Dad chimed in.

"Me, too," said Mom.

"Me three," I said, then turned to John. "Now you're supposed to say, *Me four.*"

To which he replied, "I like sushi better."

Mom and Dad had come along for support. Mom was more open about her worries and fears. She wanted the whole thing to be over already.

Dad tried to lighten the mood by discussing sports with John. "Say, John, do you have any interest in going to Santa Anita raceway tomorrow?" he asked.

"I can't. There's a Red Sox game," John answered.

"Those bums?" Dad said, egging him on.

"They're my team, I've got to support 'em," he said as we pulled into the parking lot.

I couldn't wait to be sitting on the patio at Orso's. I was anxious about the whole thing. What was my surgeon going to say? Just going back to the hospital put my stomach in knots. As we took the elevator down to the cancer center, my legs got weak and I felt nauseous. I was walking very slowly in those days, but tried to maintain good posture. I asked my folks to sit in the waiting room, where the aquarium was, while I had my exam.

When Doctor #9's nurse put me on the scale, I weighed in about four or five pounds lighter. "That's all?" I exclaimed. I couldn't believe it. I'd felt sure that discarding all those unwanted body parts would mean at least ten. I felt anxious as we entered the examining room. I didn't like it there. It was small and sterile. No windows, fluorescent lighting, and completely lacking in comfort or warmth.

The nurse checked my blood pressure, my pulse, and my temperature. So far, so good. I was handed a hospital gown to change into as I neatly placed my clothes on the chair next to the examining table. There was restraint to my movements. I just wanted to be putting on my clothes again and leaving. The doctor entered, cheerful as ever. She offhandedly mentioned a tabloid. "I don't know about you, but I got a kick out of being in there," she said. That was the first time a tabloid had ever been mentioned to me. Up until that moment I'd no idea the story had run anywhere but in the article Elaine showed me in the hospital. Well, I guess that made it official. Everyone knew I'd had cancer, and everyone knew I'd undergone a hysterectomy. Nothing to be ashamed of—still, it made me self-conscious and embarrassed. It all felt too personal to be so public.

As I lay down on the table and placed my feet in the stirrups, the nurse drew the curtain closed, separating me from John. I tried to detach myself from what was happening. I closed my eyes as Doctor #9 penetrated me with her fingers, feeling for abnormalities in both my vaginal and anal cavities. I wanted to get out of there so badly, but she continued to poke and prod as if she were an auto mechanic looking under the hood.

"Any trouble urinating?" she asked.

"No."

"Diarrhea? Constipation?"

"No. No. I've experienced some light pink staining after intercourse," I said, hating that John was on the other side of the curtain. I hadn't wanted him to know that things weren't completely back to normal sexually. In truth, nothing was back to normal, sexually or otherwise.

"You've had sex already?"

"You said I could."

"No, it's fine. I mean, it's great that your libido is strong." Lying there, I wondered if it was my libido or my need to be a normal woman that had fueled my desire. Then she added, "It's probably just the scar tissue from where we sewed you up. Give it another ten days and then try again."

Doctor #9 took some tissue samples for biopsy, pulled off her gloves, and told me to get dressed as she reopened the curtain and sat down in the chair. That was when she said it. "I've been giving it some thought, and I think you should consider radiation treatment," she blurted out. *What did she just say? Did she just use the R word?*

My heart sank as this emotional roller coaster continued. "You said everyone thought I was clean and no post-op treatment was necessary," I insisted. Why had she said one thing and then taken it back? What had changed?

"I know, but I just wasn't completely comfortable, so I called a colleague of mine in Wisconsin who specializes in uterine cancer. Wisconsin is the fattest state in the union, and because of all the obesity in women there they have an extremely high number of cases," she rattled off. "Women who carry a lot of fat release higher levels of estrogen. And we all know unopposed estrogen is one of the causes of uterine cancer."

Uh-huh . . .

Then she was quick to say, "Of course, I didn't tell him it was you, simply that I had a patient whom pathology had determined to be at stage one/grade two of the disease. This colleague said he recommends radiation on all his patients. If you received the radiation, it would bring your percentage of nonrecurrence up from ninety-five to ninety-eight percent. If it were me, I'd do whatever it takes to better my odds." *If it were me?* But it wasn't her, it was *me*.

I felt like vomiting. Less than a week ago, she'd told me I was essentially cured, and I hated that she was taking it back. I hated the very idea of radiation. I'm the one who never wanted to take a simple dental X ray, and now she was pushing me into radiation? I wanted to know all the implications. What were the side effects, how long did the treatment take, and why did I need it?

"It's really up to you," she said. "If there's recurrence, it would most likely be in the vaginal cuff, so that's the only place we'd radiate." What the hell was this woman saying? I didn't even know I *had* a vaginal cuff! "Let me have you speak to the radiologist. He can answer all of your questions better than I," she said, gathering her things and exiting as John and I remained in the room.

I felt wiped out by this new turn of events. Of course, it had been Doctor #9's intention to be thorough and helpful by calling her colleague in Wisconsin. I just wish she'd thought of it before calling me to say I was cured and no further treatment was necessary. John and I waited for what seemed like an eternity but was probably half an hour. I worried about my parents in the waiting room, but we kept thinking the radiologist would be in at any moment and John wanted to be there for that. Few words were spoken as we sat and watched the clock tick.

Then the radiologist entered. His face seemed kind enough, and I was told his mother had had cancer, so he was genuine in his compassion, but there was something about him that made me uncomfortable. He wanted to examine me. There I was, already dressed and thinking we were just going to talk, but he was asking for an examination. Against my better judgment I dropped my pants again. Why did I do that? I wasn't even sure I was going to go through with it. I didn't know him, I didn't want him touching me. I felt vulnerable, violated. After a minute or so he snapped off his gloves and I quickly grabbed for my pants to get dressed.

Everything he said filled me with revulsion. The radiation procedure would occur every other week for six treatments. The first time would take the longest, maybe three hours total, and thereafter about forty-five minutes. I'd need another X ray to determine the exact location of my bladder, my bowels, and the vaginal cuff, all three of which are extremely close together. Something would be shoved up my rectum, something else up my urethra to the bladder, and then the radiating wand (shaped like a tampon) would be inserted into my vagina. This type of radiation is called brachytherapy.

Poor women, I thought. Is there no attention paid toward making all this stuff less humiliating? The radiologist kept talking percentages. Ninety-five percent, ninety-seven percent, first-year recurrence, third-year recurrence, blah, blah, blah. Although only one in ten women actually needs this radiation to prevent recurrence, many doctors make it standard procedure. Nine women in ten are getting radiated for nothing.

"Does the treatment have side effects?" I questioned.

His answer was hair-raising. "Possible vaginal dryness. Vaginal bleeding. Vaginal shrinkage."

"Vaginal *shrinkage?*"

"Yes, so you must have intercourse at least twice a week to maintain its shape."

That sounded so strange to me. "What if you don't have sex all the time?" I asked.

I was startled by his response. "In some cases, the vaginal canal can shrink in length, so if you don't have regular sex, you'd have to use a dildo."

"For how long?" I asked, and the whole thing crystallized for me when he said, "The rest of your life." At that point I just shut down. I couldn't listen to all these horrible things anymore. He said I needed to heal for a few more weeks before I could begin treatment anyway, and since he was taking a vacation, I had time to think about it. Yeah, right. Have a good vacation. Thanks but no thanks, I'm outta here.

By the time I left to get my parents, two hours had passed and they were beside themselves with worry. I was completely shell-shocked, could barely speak. It all seemed so unbelievable, partly because the surgery followed so quickly on the heels of the diagnosis that we'd only lived with the notion of cancer for about a week. I'd had the operation. They'd taken everything out. That's it, it should be over. Only now, with the idea of radiation having been introduced, was the gravity of the situation fully brought home. The truth was, nothing was over.

As we sat around the tree-enclosed patio at Orso's with my parents, Rachel, and Greg, I began to cry. I'd thought it was over. I'd believed my doctor when she'd told me to "get on with my life." I didn't know the right thing to do—every alternative seemed frightening. When Elaine and Allan showed up, they were so happy and cheerful, ready to have a good lunch and toast to my good health. But within seconds they both realized something grave had happened and no one was celebrating.

"Honey, I'll call Richard for you. He's on the board at the City of Hope. Let's see who he knows," Elaine said, moving things along. And her instincts were right. This was a decision that needed to be made after I'd educated myself on it all: the brachytherapy, radiation versus no radiation, and, most important, other experts' opinions. You don't need to know someone in high places, though. Everything you need to know in terms of information is right there on the Internet. What a marvelous resource that is!

Surfing the Web

the day after my first post-op exam, Operation Brachytherapy began! I wasn't ready for the amount of energy I needed to pull off this research campaign, but what choice did I have? John immediately began surfing the Internet to find Web sites on everything. I lay in bed printing out gynecology pages from my WebTV. The goal was to gather enough knowledge so we could make an informed decision. Within no time we had hospitals, numbers, e-mail addresses, fax lines, you name it.

Elaine's friend Richard gave us the number of a head physician over at City of Hope. I put in a call to him immediately, dropped Richard's name in the message I left, and anxiously awaited his response. Camelia spoke to a few contacts in high places who all seemed to agree that for anything regarding cancer, go to Sloan-Kettering in New York or M. D. Anderson in Houston. My cousin Susan had just sold a house to a famous radiologist who said the same thing.

When the doctor from City of Hope returned my call, he very kindly gave me the names and numbers of the doctors who were the heads of gynecologic oncology at both Sloan and M. D. I thanked him profusely. He wished me luck then added, "You don't want to ask too many people, because you'll always end up with about half who tell you what you want to hear, and half who don't." Sage advice.

We placed calls and left messages everywhere. Camelia called my surgeon's nurse for the name of the doctor in Wisconsin, and also requested that they fax copies of my pathology reports to me. Whomever I spoke with was faxed those pages so they could read exactly what my condition was for their own evaluation.

Meanwhile, fresh samples from tissue removed during my surgery had been transported to Johns Hopkins (in Maryland) so that a uterine cancer pathologist could make his own determination. When Doctor #9 had asked if I wanted, at my own expense, to get a second opinion, I'd emphatically said yes, and appreciated the suggestion. Why shouldn't another expert look at it? Believe me, I felt better when the Hopkins report turned out to be exactly the same as the Cedars.

The stuff on the Internet really educated us on my type of cancer and the many different studies that had been done over the years of treatments for every different grade and stage of uterine cancer. There was no time to lose. Mom made the food we ate while John and I manned our keyboards. Over the next few days I started a file on all the information we'd gathered regarding my cancer. I went from feeling helpless to feeling empowered. In that sense the radiation treatment dilemma had its positive side. Not only did I familiarize myself with a battery of specialists who're at the top of their fields, I also gained knowledge about my disease that I'd never have obtained otherwise. It was a revelation how much info there is waiting to tap into. I'll never again get treated for even a hangnail without reading every piece of information available on the Internet.

There were Web pages full of women's personal accounts of having been through radiation therapy. A lot of them said they wished their doctors had really explained to them just how long term the side effects were. One woman complained of having painful intercourse and bleeding five years after treatment. There was also a general sense of regret that receiving the radiation prolonged feelings of sickness for years after treatment. Women who couldn't resume a normal, active sex life after surgery felt they'd made a bad situation worse.

The more I read, the less I thought the radiation was for me. The side effects seemed severe, and the only part of my body where it *might* inhibit recurrence was the vaginal cuff, where the radiation would be focused. Even that wasn't a guarantee, which was galling. Another major turnoff was that if cancer did show up somewhere else down the road, radiation was likely to be less effective the second time around.

I finally spoke with the doctor in Wisconsin whose comments had opened this whole can of worms, and was sure glad I did, because it cleared up a lot of confusion. What he explained was that follow-up appointments with your physician are key to early detection of recurrence. Many of his patients lived on farms, however—some as far as three hundred miles away—and almost none of the women continued with their follow-up examinations after their release from the hospital. Because of this, he radiated all his patients as a precautionary treatment—not so much for the nine out of ten who'd never experience recurrence, but for the one in ten who would.

In my case, he felt I was *not* a candidate as long as I was diligent about going for my checkups every three months. What a relief! Two doctors at Sloan-Kettering in New York each read my pathology reports and said adamantly that they wouldn't suggest radiation for a stage-one/grade-two patient, but each reiterated the importance of follow-up exams.

M. D. Anderson had a slightly different response. The doctor down there thought radiation on the vaginal cuff *would* be prudent, since the tumor was so low in the uterus. "The odds are already stacked in your favor, so whatever you decide, it's really a win–win situation. I don't think there's a right or wrong answer here," he said, and then referred me to a gal in radiation who specialized in brachytherapy.

When that radiologist called back, she explained that at M. D. Anderson they administer the radiation completely differently from Cedars. I found this strange. You would think there'd be a standard for this type of treatment, but there isn't. Consequently, the type of radiation treatment a patient receives will vary not only from state to state, but hospital to hospital! Who knew?

The M. D. Anderson radiologist explained that at her hospital they use a more state-of-the-art machine that is specifically designed for the vaginal cuff. This renders the other instruments for the rectum and the bladder unnecessary. Also, they don't drag it out over so many weeks. The radiologist said they'd do the treatment every other day over a period of ten days. Needless to say, if I decided to go forward with the radiation, I was going to Houston to do it. I said, "If I were your sister, what would you recommend?" Her answer was, "I'd probably say do it, but honestly, you never know what you'll do until you're actually in the situation."

So basically, I was back to square one. It was just like the doctor from City of Hope said. If I gathered too many opinions, it would just confuse me. I don't think there's a radiologist you'll ask who won't recommend radiation. Duh. But the physician at M. D. Anderson had expressed concern about how low in the uterus my tumor was. Otherwise his opinion might have leaned on the side of Sloan-Kettering.

I didn't know what to do. This was such an important decision. Elaine said I had to make a choice and once I did I had to live with it. If I didn't do the radiation, I'd have to make peace with that choice and never look back with regrets, no matter what happened down the road. I wondered if I could do that. What if a year from now they found something? Would I beat myself up that I hadn't received the radiation? On the other hand, if I got another cancer (God forbid), I could always seek radiation treatment then. Perhaps I should take my chances now?

I don't know exactly when it hit me, but I suddenly felt that 5 percent recurrence was something I could live with. Because there was 95 percent nonrecurrence on my side. What are we talking about here? Those are better odds than a motorist faces driving on the freeway, in L.A. at least! If the odds weren't so stacked in my favor, I'm sure I would have thought differently. Of course, if the situation were different, the decision might not have been left up to me in the first place. But over and over again the doctors did all agree that I would *not* be making a mistake either way.

I remember saying, "My vaginal canal is all I have left. The last thing I want to do is shrink it." Not with 95 percent in my favor. They removed my ovaries, my tubes, my uterus, my cervix, my omentum, my appendix, and forty lymph glands, and everything but the tumor itself came back negative from both pathology reports. I mean, my own body didn't seem to know it had cancer. Not from the blood tests at least.

So based on days of research and networking I was able to make an informed decision *not* to move forward with the brachytherapy. I feel like my cancer is gone and won't return. I did what was right for me. And whatever happens, I know there's no turning back.

The House of Blues

September 2000

i guess it was out of guilt that I decided to honor my commitment to walk the press line for the re-release of *This Is Spinal Tap* at the Egyptian Theater in Hollywood. I'd canceled a VH1 appearance a few months earlier when it turned out I was having the surgery that same week, and I felt bad about that.

It was hard to believe that Rob Reiner's classic mockumentary was seventeen years old, or that I was old enough to have played an adult in a movie that had been made almost two decades before. *Oy.* But I thought it might be fun, so I invited several friends to go the premiere and then to the after-party at the House of Blues.

At the risk of sounding like a diva, I found trying to figure out what outfit to wear and how to do my hair simply too much. I was exhausted just trying to camouflage my fat! Oh, the trials of being an overweight celebrity. Wasn't it enough I had cancer? Did I have to be publicly humiliated, too? Nothing fit, nothing looked good, and I just knew everyone was gonna say I looked better on *The Nanny.* Not to mention the movie from seventeen years before!

John and our friends were going to meet me at the theater, so I took the limo with Kathryn. Everyone was coming from work or wherever, so it was just the two of us. As the car drove east through bumper-to-bumper traffic, I kept flipping down the vanity mirror to check myself. Was my lipstick smudged? Was my hair still nice? I was so insecure, so ill prepared for the barrage of press I was about to face.

When Kathryn's cell phone rang, it was the public relations people advising us to kill some time before arriving, because things had gotten off to a late start and they wanted to space the celebrities' arrivals. Well, I didn't need any encouragement and told the driver to head to Elaine's house, which was nearby in the Hollywood Hills. *This will be good. She'll say something positive about the way I look and bolster my self-esteem.*

As she flung open her front door to greet us, I stood in the entryway, all smiles. "Fran, Kathryn, come on in," she said with great fanfare.

"We were early for the premiere, so I thought we'd say hello," I said in the perkiest voice I could muster.

"How wonderful. Can I offer you girls a drink?" she asked.

A drink? What about the *Fran, you look gorgeous* part? The *who did your hair? I love it!* confidence booster? I was wearing a Lacroix skirt and leather jacket with motorcycle boots, and had nearly convinced myself I looked cute. What speaks the loudest with Elaine, though, is what she doesn't say, and clearly she wasn't thrilled by what she saw. *Uh-oh. I wanna go home!* What would be the worst thing that would happen if I was a no-show? Lemme go back home, get all undressed, and back into bed where I'm happy.

But the P.R. person called Kathryn's cell phone, alerting us to come now to the theater, and I begrudgingly waddled my fat ass back into the limo. As we pulled up to the theater, I was amazed by the turnout. For an old movie, the publicity machine had managed to create a lot of hype.

The band members from Spinal Tap were halfway down the press line as I, too, began the red-carpet walk. As I passed the paparazzi, they all shouted at me.

"Fran, look over here."

"How ya feelin', Fran?"

"What's coming up next for you, Fran?"

And there I was, smiling, posing, and pretending to want to be there. *Am I holding my stomach in? Do I have lipstick on my teeth? Can I go home now?* And all the while I'm pumping, answering questions, and getting more and more exhausted with each interview. I really needed to sit down. Thank God, I hadn't worn heels!

Inside, there were people everywhere. *Is that free popcorn?* We finally settled down in our seats and began watching the film. Amazingly, it had held up well with the passing of time. I myself was surprised how cool and relevant it remained.

John and I split from the theater ahead of the crowds and dodged the reporters who were waiting for postscreening comments. We headed to the House of Blues, one of my favorite music venues in L.A. Spinal Tap was going to play. I really wished I felt better, though. Once in the limo I was really frazzled. My lipstick was off, my stomach was sore, my feet hurt. It was obvious I wasn't ready to be out in public like this yet. It was all too much for me.

At the House of Blues I worried that my friends would have a problem getting in, worried that not everyone had gotten their tickets, and worried that there wouldn't be enough table seating. What can I say? It's a thing with me, wanting everything to go smoothly for my guests. John can't believe me sometimes. As it turned out, some guests had trouble getting in, some didn't have their tickets, and there definitely wasn't enough table seating.

I sat down and began ordering food for everyone. Chicken fingers were on the menu, and I've already established my weakness for those. At the House of Blues they're especially good! Guests began to crowd around the table, shmoozing, drinking, and gabbing as the food kept coming. I'd taken a pain pill to get me through it all, but my stomach felt empty and I needed to eat. I must have scarfed down a dozen fingers in just a couple of minutes and began to watch the concert.

I remember a P.R. person, Marty, came over to my table and asked if I'd go downstairs and do an interview for a magazine show. Was he kidding? Did he realize my *kishkas* felt like they were about to drop out of me? Come on already, when is enough enough? So I said I was recovering from major surgery, and I really couldn't go downstairs. The P.R. person simply couldn't compute my response and seemed unable to hide his disappointment. He looked like he was going to cry as he disappeared into the crowd. *Nu?* Just what I needed, an emotional P.R. man to make me feel guilty.

I really was beginning to feel sick now: dizzy, sweaty, flushed, nauseous. Aren't I a fun date? I leaned over to John, told him he should stay here with all our guests but that I must get into the limo and go home. He walked me to the car that was waiting outside and put me in, instructing me to get to bed as soon as possible. No problem there; I don't know what I'd do without my bed. I love my bed. My bed was calling me. *Fran, darling, come nestle in me with the pillow and the blankie. . . .*

As I settled into the back of the limo, the driver told me there were some fans waiting for me to autograph photos. He wondered if I wanted him to pass them into the car so I could sign them. No can do! I rarely reject people, but this time I told him I really didn't feel well and needed to get home at once. With that, he snapped to it, cleared everyone away, and sped off. A man on a mission.

And it's a good thing, too, because only moments later I found myself suddenly getting green around the gills. Thank

God there was a bag of popcorn left on the seat from the movie, because just as I grabbed it, like Mount Vesuvius, I erupted. I puked so bad I can't even tell you how gross it was. Vomiting all by myself in the back of the limo. *Oy.* Sometimes there's just no glamour in being a star.

On Pins and Needles

It was a woman sunning herself by my mother's pool in Florida who said, "Tell your daughter, don't expect to be back to normal for at least six months to a year." And she was right. Mom said she was a very pretty woman with a great body who was on vacation visiting her own mom. They started chatting, and this gal revealed that she'd had the same surgery as me. In ten minutes my mom can find out anyone's life story. This woman told Mom, "There will be good days and bad days for a very long time, but then one day she'll wake up and the pain will be gone for good. Tell her to be patient."

It was reassuring to hear this from someone who'd actually been through it herself, because the surgeon kept telling me in six weeks I'd be good as new, which turned out to be a gross exaggeration. She'd told me I'd be able to go on an African safari two months after my surgery. The reality was that it had been nearly four months, and I could barely sit in a luxury car without being in pain! So I was beginning to think there was something wrong with me. Why was I taking so long to recover? Every time I'd make plans to do something, I'd end up canceling, until finally I gave up making plans at all.

As the months dragged on, John and I fell into a rut where my recovery seemed unending. We both felt stuck, afraid this was going to be the way things stayed. I, who once was so active, planning and doing all the time (we used to joke that John couldn't keep up with me), had settled into this convalescing lump. By this point I think John was just about at the end of his rope. *Trapped* is probably a more succinct way of putting just how he was feeling. It was now fifteen weeks since my surgery and we were both miserable. There was one day when I had to cancel out on yet another activity we'd planned together, and he just exploded.

"You never want to do anything!" he shouted.

"I like to do things," I said, defending myself.

"I need to get out of this house and have some fun, live my life, be with my friends, but you never want to," he accused. Poor guy had tried for so long to be patient and understanding, but in that moment he was like a champagne bottle blowing its cork.

I felt like an albatross. A monkey on his back. A ball and chain on his ankle. You name it, if it weighed ya down, I was it. I guess I wasn't as much fun as before, and I sure didn't have as much energy. The fight spiraled to a point where we wondered how we'd become so sad, so incompatible, so wrong for each other. I said meekly, "But I don't think I was like this *before* I had cancer." And then it struck us like a lightning bolt. For the first time, we could see it all clearly.

"Sweetie, you're right, this is all because you had cancer," said John. We loved each other, and there we were, fighting and blaming one another, venting our anguish and frustration, when it hit both of us that the real enemy was the cancer itself. All our current problems were because of that, not because of genuine differences. This wasn't permanent. We weren't stuck, and someday in the future things would return to the way they used to be.

We'd both felt misled about how long "getting back to normal" was going to take. John had believed the doctor's estimates and blamed me for being a bad patient. If only someone had come to my hospital room after the surgery to give me a blow-by-blow description of what to expect and what I should do throughout my recovery. A woman who'd been through it herself, like the one by my mother's pool. A person who truly knew what it felt like both emotionally and physically to have had cancer and a hysterectomy all at the same time. It's a double whammy for any gal.

The hysterectomy helps take care of the cancer problem but creates a whole new set of hormonal and reproductive issues that are permanent and irreversible. Maybe I should have considered joining a support group, but first I'd need to accept what happened and not try to deny it. Regardless, somehow the voices of women who'd been through it before managed to enter my life with some sage advice anyway. Rachel's mom, for one, turned me on to what I now consider a must-read for us all: the Harvard Women's Health Watch newsletter.

Curiously, the name of one acupuncturist kept coming up as someone worth going to. He was a medical doctor who practiced acupuncture, herb therapy, and nutrition. I swear, there must have been five different people with no connection to each other who referred me to this man.

My friend Juliette, who suffers from Crohn's disease, told me this acupuncturist, Doctor #11, saved her during her pregnancy. It was his partner and brother who helped her get pregnant in the first place. Kathryn's boyfriend, Ray, came home with a note from a coworker who'd read about my illness. She wrote to me, explaining that she'd had the same surgery as mine and hadn't begun to feel well internally until she went through her treatment with Doctor #11. Well, I don't need to get hit over the head with a hammer to wake up, so I called his office in Santa Monica and made an appointment in the hope he'd be able to speed up my recovery. I was ready to start enjoying life again.

I drove myself over, and believe me, driving still wasn't easy. The seat belt hurt my incision, and the bumps rattled my insides. As I entered Doctor #11's waiting area, there was beautiful Asian-sounding music playing on the sound system. Several people of varying ages sat and waited for their appointments. One wall was covered with books on nutrition, Taoism, and Buddhism, as well as gift boxes of Doctor #11's special tea blends and herbs.

The nurse brought me into Doctor #11's office, where I sat and waited. I enjoyed looking at the photos and knickknacks displayed on the shelf unit and desk. Small traces of the doctor's private world painted a picture of him. There were framed photos of a beautiful-looking family I assumed to be his. Diplomas and serene Asian art hung on the wall. The furnishings were sparse and simple in their design.

When he entered his office, he was younger than I thought he'd be, and extremely soft-spoken. Everything about him was calming. He shook my hand as he introduced himself and seemed extremely compassionate as I talked about my cancer and the surgery. He nodded his head as he listened. I studied his kind face, the shirt he wore, his white coat, and his wedding ring. *Is he this tranquil at home?*

He told me to stop eating nightshade vegetables. I'd never heard of nightshade vegetables, but they sounded awful, and I was sure I'd never eaten anything like that. Well, it turns out they're tomatoes, potatoes, peppers, and eggplants, all of which I managed to eat plenty of. I love Italian food, need I say more? "These vegetables do most of their growing at night, hence the name *night-*

shade vegetables," he explained. "And they're considered inflammatories. If you have arthritis or any kind of inflammation, be it post-operative or a simple sprain, you should avoid these foods." Who knew?

He also took me off starches like pasta and white rice and suggested I eat brown rice instead. "No pasta?" I exclaimed. "But I love pasta. I eat it almost every day!"

"Too hard to digest. No dairy, no sugar, nothing raw like salads, and very little animal protein," he rattled off. *This guy is nuts.*

"How 'bout fruits?" I asked, hopefully.

"No fruit. Except for apples," was his reply. *Oy. How is this man going to make me feel any better when I'm starving to death?* "And here's a special tea that you have to brew and drink after every meal," he said, handing me a bag of twigs and bark that looked like it came from his driveway. *Am I supposed to drink this stuff or use it as fertilizer?*

"Oh well, I guess I have nothing to lose," I said, acquiescing. I'd spent four months feeling lousy, and I was desperate. He promised he'd make me feel much better in six to eight weeks if I were to come for treatment every week and follow his nutritional guides.

He looked at my tongue and felt my pulse. That was the exam: the tongue, the wrist, and done. Normally, I would have considered this exam a joke, but instead I found myself totally mesmerized.

The next thing I knew I was in a private room on a padded table that had clean white paper pulled across it. The tranquil sounds of wind chimes and delicate instruments filled my ears. A black-and-white photo of a bowl of noodles in a rustic Asian café hung on the wall.

He began to stick the acupuncture needles into me quickly, precisely, and, most important, painlessly. Now, I'd never been into acupuncture. The one time I'd tried it in the past, it hurt. *Duh, the dude is sticking needles into me*—what did I expect? That said, this doctor was part of a Chinese family who'd been practicing for generations and he made the experience most pleasant. He inserted a few needles in each calf, in my abdomen, my chest, my head, and my hands. "Don't move," he instructed, as he turned on a heat lamp and let its warmth penetrate my stomach. Oh, did I ever enjoy that. Then he placed a long string through my fingers and said if I had any problems to pull the string and someone would come right in to help. The light in the room was subdued and the music serene. Now, I don't know if I needed any of that stuff to make the needles work, but it sure helped to make me relax.

After that, I continued going week in and week out. Doctor #11 was always interested in what was going on in my life: Was I happy? Was my relationship good? Was my sex life satisfying? I'd really never had a doctor take such a personal interest in me before. Even though a part of me wondered if he was taking notes for the tabloids, I preferred to think this was the way good doctors should be and leave it at that.

I listened to Doctor #11's words as if they were gospel. By the end I was sold hook, line, and sinker. An absolute skeptic in the beginning, I wound up falling in love. I was buying the CDs that always wafted over the sound system, the herbs, and, per the doctor's instructions, I tried to take brisk walks every day. Soon enough, I began to feel better. Good ol' Doctor #11 always asked how John was, and held me in his arms when I wept about the cancer. He was the closest thing to Marcus Welby I'd ever experienced, and I do believe he helped me. Plus, he was a medical doctor, so my insurance picked up the tab. Acupuncture had turned out to be a good thing now that I'd found the right physician, and in combination with walking, diet, and herbs it became the formula that put my recovery on the right path.

You never know when a pearl will drop in your lap, so stay open and you, too, may get a note through a friend from someone you don't even know—one that will make all the difference. . . .

Melinda

i don't exactly know when it hit me, but it was definitely a few months into my recovery that I realized I'd be living the rest of my life as a woman who'll never be pregnant. It was difficult to accept, even for me, who hadn't had a lifelong burning desire to be pregnant. I can only imagine how those women who've always wanted to have a baby, but now can't, must feel.

It wasn't fair. I hated that this was foisted on me. Especially since through therapy I was finally understanding my indifference to having a baby and actually becoming more receptive to the idea. Needless to say, the timing of it all was highly ironic. All the years I *could* have had a baby I was frightened of the idea and didn't. If I'd ever tried, I would have become aware of my luteal phase defect, because I would have miscarried due to low progesterone levels. I'd have figured it out then, and I never would have gotten the cancer.

But psychologically, I wasn't near ready, and probably never would have been if I hadn't gotten such good therapy when my marriage was coming apart. So I'd figured out why I didn't want to have a baby, and now that I did, I couldn't. *C'est la vie!* I decided to be fatalistic about it all. I don't need to get pregnant or become a mother to have a rich, full life. For that matter, if I want to have a baby, I don't have to carry it to be its mother. John said we didn't need to have a biological baby to have a family. He's an extremely generous man and I love him for having said that. But for a while there, I gotta admit, it was difficult to grasp the permanence of it all, and I found myself slipping into a depression.

I never expected to find what I needed where and when I did. It was at a baby shower, which I really didn't want to go to in the worst way. I mean, I didn't like going to baby showers when I *had* a uterus. But that was where I met Melinda. The shower was for Juliette, one of the gals who'd recommended my acupuncturist, and it was on November 4. For most people that's a date of little significance, but November 4 happened to be the anniversary of my wedding to Peter. So this shower was a real *zetz* for me—on my way to Juliette's, *divorce* and a *hysterectomy* were all I could think about. If it weren't for Camelia's having been invited, too, I'm sure I wouldn't have gone.

But I felt it was time to resurface, and Juliette, whom I've known since her producing days years ago at MTV, knows everyone in Hollywood. So I agreed to go. I wanted to look good, strong, and healthy for all to see. After careful deliberation, I finally settled on some really cool lizard-print pants and cowboy boots with a cashmere sweater.

Juliette, a warm and vivacious Englishwoman, was beaming with joy as she welcomed us at the door with a huge belly, smiling from ear to ear. She looked beautiful. I was trying my best to forget the divorce and hysterectomy, mingling and getting acquainted, when Juliette called over a woman and said, "Fran, I want you to meet Melinda. She had the same surgeon as you and the same surgery, too." Could the party get any worse?

Melinda and I looked at each other and exchanged uncomfortable hellos. *Add salt to the wound, why don't you?* There we were,

Melinda and I, the hysterectomy girls, who hadda visit our on-cologist every three months to check for cancer recurrence, standing among a sea of pregos, women with children, and healthy career gals. We shook hands and drifted off in different directions.

The food at the shower was light and ladylike with tea, scones, and finger sandwiches—very English. And the company was good. But then the dreaded opening of the gifts began. Even under normal circumstances, I always found this part of a baby shower notori-ously boring by the fifth present. Now, with what I was going through, this gift-opening ritual was sheer and absolute torture.

I graciously "oohed" and "ahhed" as Juliette displayed each adorable little baby outfit. A play suit, a jumper, T-shirts, booties—on and on it went. As the pile of wrapped gifts dwindled down to the last few, I decided I wanted to talk to this gal, Melinda, ask her what she thought about our surgeon, Doctor #9.

I saw her standing in the doorway to the kitchen, keeping a safe distance from everything. It seemed like this ritual was hard for her, too. So I got up and walked into the kitchen to talk to her. "I just wanted to ask you, did our surgeon remove your appen-dix . . . and forget to tell you?"

"You, too?" she responded.

It was like meeting a kindred spirit. Of course, her situation was completely different. She'd gone in to have outpatient surgery for an ovarian cyst, and it wasn't until she was out cold on the table that they realized her condition was much more serious. She had ovarian cancer. The doctors ran to Joe, her husband, in the waiting room to have him sign papers for what turned out to be life-altering inpatient surgery.

Anyway, we both said we hated the idea of going to some cancer support group to talk about our "feelings." Ugh. The thought of it made us both squirm. I'm sure it's very helpful for most people, but I think Melinda and I were still in denial mode and just wanted to blend back into normal life as if nothing had happened.

Like magnets, we connected in that kitchen at Juliette's baby shower and immediately became our own support group of two. Melinda is a bright, intelligent woman with a happy, gummy smile. She's an artist whose husband, Joe, is a television producer. I know in this life there are angels that guide us. Just like in that Wim Wenders movie *Wings of Desire*, Melinda and I were destined to meet. What we both needed, we found in each other. And how's this for bizarre: We had the same surgery, the same surgeon, and we were both born on the same day, September 30. Is that weird or what?

We exchanged e-mail addresses and began writing at once. It was like finding a life raft in a sea where everybody knows how to swim but you. What a relief and what a gift she became. After weeks of writing we decided to take a walk together on the beach. But what if we proved better pen pals than actual mates? We might blow the wonderful support we were getting through our e-mails if we suddenly decided we didn't like each other. Well, life is all about taking risks, so we forged ahead with it.

When she arrived at my house, I hugged her at the door for a long time. Although I hadn't actually seen her since that brief encounter at the shower, our e-mails were extremely personal, so I felt a strange and deep connection. I liked her. I did not, however, remember the wonderful, hearty laugh she had. All I said was, "Welcome," and she threw back her head and let out a huge guffaw, which was music to my ears. I was glad we'd taken this next step.

Once, when Melinda and I were on a walk, we spotted two women on the same road pushing babies in those three-wheeled jogging strollers about three hundred yards ahead. Two women with babies and two hollowed-out women with *no* babies.

I don't know why, but I wanted to pass them to get ahead. I didn't like trailing behind them. There was too much symbolism lurking there—the distance from us to them, and the fact that they had kids and we didn't. All I could think of was beating them, passing them, putting them behind me.

So I started to jog, pulling Melinda along with me. She didn't feel the same urgency, but humored me just the same. Huffing and puffing, we forged ahead as the two unsuspecting mothers with children fast-walked, gabbing along their merry way. It sounds crazy, but it meant *everything* to me to win that race—a race no one was running but me. F.Y.I.—I did get ahead of them, and as I did, I raised my arms like a victorious marathon runner.

When Melinda reached her two-year anniversary of good health, it was me and John whom she and Joe wanted to celebrate with. Over delicious Italian food, we raised our glasses and toasted to Melinda's good health, my good health, and the men in our lives who'd stood by us and lived through it with us. Our heroes. Joe appreciated this and began to open up about how scared he was when he stood alone signing that paper for Melinda's hysterectomy in the hospital waiting room. Our hearts went out to him and how he must have felt. That night our support group of two became four.

Chester Drescher

a fter my surgery I was never the same, and my beloved Chester Drescher was never the same, either. When I returned from the hospital he just couldn't accept the change in me. He was so old already. At eighteen years he was finally running out of steam.

The one thing I was careful not to do was bend down to lift things. The surgeon had told me to avoid this, and I did. But try explaining that to your dog who's so used to being picked up and carried everywhere. Poor old guy, what a deep bond we shared. I always said, "When this little guy goes, he's going to leave a hole in my life the size of the Grand Canyon."

Having an old dog is like being in the company of any geriatric. They get all the same afflictions. The hearing goes, the eyesight goes, arthritis sets in, and it's all downhill from there. How sad it is that a turtle can live to 150, or a parrot can live as long as a human, but man's best friend can only live for a decade or two. With some things there's little justice.

My great-grandmother in her last years used to say, "It's no good to get old." I think that's where Chester was at, too.

In his day, boy, he was such the little star. On magazine covers with me, in movies, on talk shows. He even had a recurring role on *The Nanny*. He was always right in the thick of it. Always with that photogenic smile, right by my side. He was a one-woman dog and I loved him for that.

At first I'd seen my recovery as a good thing because it forced me to be home a lot with Chester. We were always in bed together. But toward the end my condition robbed me of the energy I needed to keep him completely comfortable. He was becoming incontinent and had bouts where his kidneys were acting sluggish and he just wouldn't feel well. But then he'd have his good days, like when I shot the cover of *Rosie* magazine.

Rosie O'Donnell and I have been friends for many years. We met shooting the movie *Car 54, Where Are You?* I don't know why, but some of my best friends come out of my worst movies. When she learned about my cancer, she called my parents immediately. She was on hiatus and I guess really out of the loop, because it was about two months after my surgery when she surfaced. I'm sure she still holds a lot of pain from the loss of her mother, who died from breast cancer, and hearing about my struggles made her very upset.

When she called me, I told her the whole story from the beginning. It was nice to speak with such openness and friendship. It had been too long, and that phone call from her was another positive thing to come out of the cancer.

Rosie and I began e-mailing each other after that first conversation, sharing the lives we were each living now. And it wasn't long before she asked me to tell my cancer story in the premiere issue of *Rosie* magazine. Up to this point I hadn't wanted to do any press on the subject, but Rosie was different; she was a friend. I trusted her to handle my story with sensitivity. As it turned out the most daunting aspect of it all was shooting the cover, even though she offered to fly to L.A. and make it as easy on me as possible.

Thanks to Rosie, the magazine accommodated all my needs. We shot the cover in my home, and didn't do the interview until the next day. Tommy Hilfiger supplied my clothes, and my friend Gregory did the makeup. Nothing fancy; Rosie wanted everything very real and natural.

Knowing well in advance that I was going before cameras for the first time since my operation, I tried to watch what I ate and exercise a bit more. But it wasn't easy finding a type of exercise that didn't leave me feeling like hell the next day. I know about "no pain, no gain," but this was ridiculous. There were times I couldn't stand up straight. I tried yoga, walking, swimming, and—foolishly—even hiking. But everything I tried left me with an inflamed abdomen. Finally I said, "Forget it! I'd rather have a fat ass and feel good." How liberating. All my life I'd felt guilty if I didn't exercise, but now I couldn't. Hooray! For the time being I'd allow myself to *let it all hang out*. Whoo-hoo!

In the weeks that preceded the shoot, Chester was not doing well. Often I'd think of my grandmother Yetta, caring for her mother, Esther, who lived with my grandparents for many, many years. In Esther's youth she was a great help to Yetta, cooking, cleaning, and, most important, helping to raise the children (my mother and her sister, Denise). But when she got very old, the tables turned and the daughter became the mother.

I was beginning to feel like a martyr. The love I'd felt for Chester and he for me throughout the years is what drove me to get up throughout the night, tending to his needs, spoon-feeding him and cleaning his bedding. I swore I'd never put Chester to sleep, that in the end I'd hold him and comfort him until it was all over. That was the beautiful fantasy I had for Chester. But life always gets in the way of fantasies, and a whole different scenario unfolded.

In the meantime, the day of the *Rosie* shoot, miraculously,

Chester was in rare form. It was as if he was stimulated and excited by the crew and all the activity. He loved being on a set, and that day was a happy one for him. After almost nineteen years of being a real ham in front of the camera, this was to be his last photo shoot. He lived for only one week longer, during which he went into a rapid decline.

John and I came home Christmas night and found Chester unable to get up, covered in his own feces. Now, this was an extremely dignified and very proud dog. So to see him in this helpless and humiliating condition was clear evidence that he'd reached his limit. My heart ached for the misery he must've felt in that very old body of his. I bathed him in warm water in my bathroom sink, but moments after, he began yelping in pain. It was so scary and frightening.

Because it was Christmas, no one was at our regular vet, so I ran to my medicine chest, ground up some medication, and stuck it in ice cream for him to lick up. Within minutes, his tiny body relaxed and went to sleep. I, on the other hand, got no sleep, jumping out of bed every ten minutes with each movement or moan he made. My best hope was to keep him sedated, hydrated, and nourished until we figured out what to do.

By morning, nothing had changed and I finally accepted that things would never get better, but only worse and worse. He was not sick, he was old, he'd never get well. Never.

On December 26, 2000, the worst year of my life got even worse. I called the vet and we agreed that she'd come to the house in the late afternoon and put Chester down. I felt an eerie calm that day. It was as though I had a window of clarity and had to follow through.

Chester and I lay on the bed together all day. I kept him very relaxed on Valium and I just kissed and stroked him. I whispered in his ear how much I loved him. I'd always said, "There'll never be another you," and I repeated it over and over that day. We had penne pasta together. He seemed to want it and I didn't want to deny him anything. He really couldn't digest stuff like that anymore, but it didn't matter.

It was a beautiful, sunny day and I held him outside on my deck. I wanted him to feel the sun on his face and the wind in his hair one more time. I inhaled his scent and brushed him and cradled him. When the doctor arrived it seemed too soon, and I wanted to send her away, but what was going to change?

At least today we had closure, calmness, and beautiful, quiet loving moments. Really, it was the way we should all go. I held Chester in my arms while he ate a plate of chocolate ice cream. I don't think he had an awareness that there was another person in the room with us. He was so into the ice cream. My darling Chester Drescher, the greatest dog in the world, gently received his injection, which he hardly seemed to notice, while eating chocolate ice cream in his mama's arms.

———————

I was so devastated by my loss I wrote this poem. I'm sharing it with you not because I'm contemplating a new career as a poet, but rather because I wrote it from the heart, and it seemed a richly deserved homage to my wonderful Chester.

Ode to Chester

I now feel so empty and cold. . . .

the twenty-sixth of December,
a day I'll always remember.
no words can be spoken,
to mend a heart that is broken.
my house is no longer a home.

oh, but my sadness is deep
I bravely, courageously put my Chester to sleep.
no more barks in the hallways,
my love lives for him always.
I've saved tufts of fur from his comb.

now drowned are my fears,
by my oceans of tears.
and long will I miss
his bright smile, his kiss.
I pray he is free now to roam.

after nineteen years, it still came too soon.
north star, orange sky, crescent moon.
the night could not have been clearer,
and I thought to myself, *it's the end of an era*. . . .
the angels cashed in on their loan.

New Year's, 2001

It had not been a good year to say the least. In fact it stunk, who's kidding whom? First it was the cancer, and then poor ol' Chester. What's next, a tsunami? Oh, the guilt I felt over putting that dog down. I got so depressed over the emptiness of my life that I felt like a tragic figure in an old movie. Did you see *Anna Karenina*? Picture her with my voice.

I was determined to make 2001 a better year, filled with happier, healthier times. So John and I decided that for New Year's we'd go to a spa for some R&R. I've gone to spas on a few occasions, and I must say, it can be quite the lovely getaway. Of course, I don't go nuts trying to lose weight or anything. I never even set foot on a scale. That would only ruin my vacation. No, no, I go for the pampering and the rest.

It's great, you never have to get out of your sweats, never have to wear makeup, don't even have to speak if you don't want to—sounded right up my alley. So we headed to the Rancho La Puerta, just across the Mexican border. There they'd do it all for me. Feed me, walk me, meditate and massage me. That's all I asked.

We drove from L.A. down to Mexico, listening to sports on the radio the whole time. Upon arrival, we followed the signs to the main registration building, where the valet took our car. After check-in, we were led to the clubhouse for orientation and scheduling of classes and treatments for the week. This was more complicated and stressful than I'd anticipated.

"You can't do a hot stone massage until Thursday," a heavy-set woman named Yolanda said as she sat behind her computer monitor.

"What? You mean to tell me I'm not getting the hot stone massage today? I just drove three and a half hours listening to sports the entire way and I need those hot rocks," I whined, slightly losing it.

"A dried herb wreath-making class is all I can work out for today," she said. "But it's very relaxing," she added, while typing into her keyboard as she read the spa treatment schedule.

"I'll take it, but I'm very disappointed," I answered, collecting my itinerary and map of the grounds. We studied those maps in earnest but still couldn't navigate our way through the maze of walkways and paths that wound around the premises.

"We have to go this way to get to the Casa Del Sol casitas," John insisted as we stood at a fork in the road.

"That way? That's the El Encanto Calle casitas." We never agree on directions, and this place was like our worst nightmare. "Where the hell is Casa Del Sol?" I said, getting nervous and desperately in need of a hot bath. Around and around we walked, passing the clubhouse at least three times, until finally, after having exhausted every possible option, we ended up at our casita.

The porch light was off and it was hard to find the keyhole. I was hating this place and wondering if we'd made the right choice. Then we opened the door, and like Dorothy arriving in Oz, everything turned Technicolor.

It was a rustic little house, and it was beautiful. "This is nice," I said, as I dropped my suitcase and pounced on the bed. The cozy living room was decorated with Mexican-style furnishings, lots of wrought iron, glazed tiles, and colorful fabrics. There was a wood-burning fireplace, a huge king-size bed, a big bathroom, and a lush private patio. I loved it and immediately shifted gears.

While filling up the bathtub I unpacked my stuff. My electric toothbrush, some sundries, my hiking boots, a few sweats, a few sweaters. Oh yeah, and Chester's cremation urn. What? He always liked to travel. I hoped the TV had at least one English-language channel. "Where's the TV?" I asked John.

"No TV," he answered, as he sat at the edge of the bed listening to the crackling reception of his football game from a small clock radio on his nightstand.

"*No TV?* How could that be? I'm going to call someone at the reception desk," I said, flustered.

"No phones," he answered, never once breaking his stare at the radio.

"No phones, too?" I responded, flabbergasted. "Well, what am I supposed to do without a phone or a TV?" I added, feeling panicked by the prospect of a whole week without either of my little friends.

"Read," he answered. John always becomes monosyllabic when a game is on.

"*Read?* For a whole *week?*" Was he crazy? By now I was incensed. I mean, I was talking to a back in front of a radio. "I can't deal with this now, I'm late for my wreath-making class," I said in a huff, grabbing my map and heading for the crafts hacienda. Wherever the hell that was.

Exactly thirty-seven minutes later, and after three completely contradictory sets of directions from guests more relaxed than myself, I accidentally happened upon the crafts hacienda, which turned out to be above the dining room. Well, why didn't they say so? The dining room was the one building whose location I'd made sure to know!

As I entered the classroom, I saw about a dozen women gathered around a long worktable piled high with dried herbs, leaves, and flowers. Outside of those women-in-prison documentaries,

I'd never seen so many frumpy-looking ladies all in one place before. Now, there's no makeup, and then there's *no* makeup. Not even a little under-eye concealer! And the hair, all a mess! Their clothes looked like stuff you'd wear to do laundry. Oh, come on, wasn't there anything cuter than that in their closets? There's no way these gals could've possibly been here with their husbands or boyfriends.

The teacher, an older woman who looked like she was part Native American, came running up to me. "Hello and welcome, grab yourself a Styrofoam doughnut and start choosing your herbs," she said cheerfully. Just as I reached for the piece of Styrofoam, she was back in my face. "That'll be twenty-five dollars," she said extending the open palm of her hand.

"What do you mean, twenty-five dollars? I thought everything was included?" I asked, slightly taken aback.

"Not this. Wreath making is extra," she said, as she clamped her turquoise-and-silver-ringed fingers around the doughnut.

"But I didn't bring my purse, I only brought my room key and map," I explained.

"I'll lend you the money," said some perky blonde with a Chicago accent.

"Oh, that's very sweet of you," I said, as the teacher relinquished her hold on the doughnut. "Where's your casita? I'll bring you the cash right after class," I offered, always hating to owe people money.

"Don't worry about it. I'll see you in the dining room sometime over the week," she answered, and resumed tending to her creation. She certainly seemed relaxed; everyone did. Was I the only new kid on the block still wearing my badge of big-city hypertension?

I noticed I displayed more aggression than my Zen'd-out sisters as I grabbed for this branch of eucalyptus and that bunch of sage before any of the other gals could get their grubby little paws on them. I had to calm down, I was being too result-oriented. This was about the art of putting it together for the sheer pleasure of it. This experience was about focusing on the smell, the feel, the creative and meditative aspects of making what is essentially an ugly, cheap-looking wreath you're never gonna wanna put in your home anyway.

Wreath in hand, I managed to retrace my way back to our casita. Proudly displaying my creation above the fireplace mantel, I noticed I was feeling a bit more relaxed.

At mealtime, John and I marched ourselves over to the dining room. Vegetables and more vegetables were the plat du jour. Bottles of Beano lining the buffet tables served as a warning we were in for one gassy vacation. Let me just say, the sounds that flew out of people in yoga class the next morning I'd never heard in my life!

The daily regimen being what it was, I began to develop a taste for stir-fried vegetables with tofu. "Where's the rice?" I asked at one point, feeling deprived.

"No rice," the server replied. Well, it doesn't get much plainer than that. I would have enjoyed rice, but I asked, and that was my answer, "no rice," and I learned to live without it. Meanwhile, my constitution was better than ever. Normally, I'm lucky if I go to the bathroom once a day, but there, I was going at least two or three times!

Each morning a bunch of seventy-year-olds and I strolled through the gardens. I chose the less challenging hikes. No point in pushing myself, only to end up bedridden the next day with abdominal cramps. One afternoon I signed up for a forty-five-minute sunset hike. My hair was freshly washed, my face scrubbed clean. No makeup for me anymore, not even lipstick. There I was with about six other women and the guide as we walked through the grounds of the ranch, through the herbs, the labyrinth, and the meditation center. It was a beautiful late afternoon. The sun was warm and golden and the mountains looked majestic on the horizon. How lovely it all was; how relaxed I'd become.

One woman realized she'd forgotten to change out of her tennis shoes and into her hiking boots. She was so distressed she finally decided to run back to her casita to get them and then catch up with us. Personally, I didn't see what she was so concerned about. We really weren't doing anything that required hiking boots anyway. *Famous last words.* As we reached the foothills of the mountain, it struck me that it wasn't so much majestic as mammoth.

"Are we going up this mountain?" I asked in panic. "I'm recovering from surgery, are we going *all* the way up? Does anybody want to bail and go back with me?" I wished it had been a bit easier to find my way around that place, or I would have simply split on my own. But I pictured myself wandering for miles in the Mexican foothills before getting arrested by the border patrol.

With that, the woman who'd gone back to retrieve her hiking boots caught up with us. She was huffing and puffing from her run to and fro, all enthusiastic about this mountain we were about to tackle. No wonder she wanted her hiking boots; that mountain was *huge.* Everyone was encouraging me to forge ahead. The instructor said it really wasn't all that difficult and that we'd take it very slow. If I wasn't the loser in the group, I don't know who was. Since my surgery I'd grown afraid of the pain I'd feel if I pushed myself, but the other gals seemed so supportive, I decided it was do or die. I'd take the challenge and scale that mountain.

I remember it being extremely windy in certain spots. I mean, like if you weren't careful you might blow off the mountain altogether. Fortunately, there were points of interest along the way that allowed me to stop and rest as the leader went on and on about this Indian carving and that edible berry.

One woman had a camera and was snapping shots of everything. *Oh, come on—haven't you seen a berry before?* At a particularly glorious spot, which offered a view of the land far below us, she asked if I'd be so kind as to take a picture. I, of course, said yes, being the accessible star I am.

"Who's going to take it?" I asked.

"You," she replied, shoving the camera in my hands. *Nu?* So I snapped a lovely shot of her in front of the view and handed back the camera. I hope it came out okay.

This was not a "45-minute hike," as I'd misread, but a "4.5-mile" one that took about two hours to complete. By the time I got back I was so beat I can't even tell you. My feet were sore and I needed a massage pronto. John couldn't believe I'd actually climbed that mountain, but I had!

That evening when we headed for the dining room, I ran into that nice lady from Chicago and returned the twenty-five dollars she'd lent me for my herb wreath, which, incidentally, had not only grown on me, but was coming home with me, too. Anyway, the mess hall smelled particularly delicious and I just couldn't wait to dig in. Oh man, I could've eaten a horse, but instead devoured a double helping of broccoli rabe, tofu, and, at long last, rice. *Mmmm.*

Now, here's the incredible thing about it all. The next morning I felt no pain from the hike. I mean, none. It was like awakening from a sleep. I'd turned a corner and could now start pushing myself more. The woman by my mother's pool was right!

One afternoon toward the end of the week, just as I was sprinting over to my posture class, I ran into a gal wearing a full face of makeup, jewelry, and wedgies, holding her map and seeming quite frazzled. "Excuse me, I'm lost, can you show me how to get to the clubhouse?" she asked, sounding kinda desperate.

In braided pigtails, Chapstick, and baggy sweats, I looped my arm in hers, smiled broadly, and said, "Come on, I'll take you there. . . ."

Paris

Mid-January 2001

When John and I returned home after our spa experience, I felt really relaxed. That is, until John dropped a bomb. "I want to start going back to my apartment a couple of nights a week now that you're better," he said casually, while folding his laundry.

"*Wha—?*" I couldn't hide my surprise, it came so out of left field. "I mean, do whatever's good for you," I lied. Shit, fuck, somewhere along the line, between my cancer and the dog's dying, I'd allowed myself to become codependent again. John was the caregiver and I was the patient. I felt safe around him and now suddenly he wanted his old life back? I mean, it had only been six months of hell, couldn't he hang in a little longer?

But like a baby bird, it was time to be pushed out of the nest. Whatever relaxed feeling I'd taken back from the spa left with John as he flung his duffel bag of clean clothes over his shoulder and walked out the door.

"'Bye, darling. I love you, I'll see you in a couple of days," I said cheerfully, waving good-bye. *Mean ol' John! What's his big rush anyway?* As I triple-locked the door and armed the alarm, I felt strangely alone. I mean, before I got sick, John and I used to enjoy being alone a few days out of each week, and I was proud of that. It was something I'd learned to like and liked to learn. I would catch up with friends, read, write, or just enjoy being in my home. What had changed? What was different? Something was missing. And then it hit me. No Chester.

Throughout the years I'd struggled to conquer my fears, find myself, and become independent, not one single day was experienced without Short Stuff. Without a man, yes, but never without Chester. He was a constant presence in my life for almost nineteen years, and I don't think I fully felt the emptiness his passing had created until John was gone, too. *Oy.* I needed this like a hole in the head.

Or maybe it was *exactly* what I needed, because after I bellowed like a baby, kicking and screaming my way through every room in the house, I'd suddenly had enough. I became sick of myself. Whatta crybaby, whatta loser, what an infant! *Shut the fuck up and cut it the hell out!* I said to myself. I always snap to it when I give myself a stiff talking-to. For God's sake, there I was with a wonderful man, a beautiful home, my health back, and both my parents still alive, as well as my grandmother, who's still smoking half a pack a day down in Florida! Even the dog had lived for nearly two decades, so what was I whining about? Who *was* this drama queen? I could no longer recognize myself.

And what must I have seemed like to John? This downtrodden woman with one problem after another. First the cancer, then the dog, when do we get to be happy again? When do we get to enjoy life? That was it; I was not going to indulge this any longer. I needed to clear my head, stop being the patient, and get my mojo back.

So I did what any self-respecting out-of-work sitcom star would do. I cashed in some frequent flier mileage and all by myself left for Paris. I was both scared and exhilarated to board the plane, but something told me this was what I needed to break out of my rut, so I took a deep breath and dived in.

I don't know what it is about that place, but it always makes me feel good when I'm there. I have a great time, even though I don't speak a word of French. Well, actually, I do speak "menu." I can order in a restaurant like a pro. Can you say *pommes frites?* Self-preservation, baby, I gotta eat, don't I?

Now, I've been to Paris both rich and poor, but it really makes no difference, because for me the heart and soul of the city is experienced in the simple things. They have vendors on street corners making fresh crêpes, which they spread chocolate on, fold up, and hand you all hot and melty for just a few francs. Trust me, it's heaven on earth. The smell alone is worth the whole trip. And I love walking my feet off. Gimme a map and a box of Band-Aids and I'm all set!

Chester and I went to Paris together years ago. It was a dream come true for both of us. Some women cherish memories of great love affairs they had in the City of Lights. Me? I cherish memories of being there with Chester Drescher. What's the matter? Believe me, when we strolled together down Boulevard Saint-Germain it was plenty romantic! There we'd be, dining together at Brasserie Lipp, gorging ourselves on soufflés and table scraps. Ah, those were the days.

As it turned out, many of my friends would be in Paris the same time as I. My photographer friend from New York, Roxanne, was covering the couture fashion shows, and she invited me to go to all the ones she was working. I'd never done anything like that before. It sounded so glamorous and exciting.

The first show (unveiling the work of an Italian designer who shall remain nameless) took place at a large warehouse complex on the outskirts of town. Hundreds of ladies were arriving at the same time, wearing big fur coats and heavy perfume. *I guess this is the place*, I thought as I began to merge with the crowd, trying to act like I belonged. Clinging to the invitation Roxanne arranged for me, I showed it to an usher, who then led me to a seat. The chairs were so petite and the winter coats were so bulky, everyone crushed together shoulder to shoulder. I pulled my arms out of my sleeves, elbowing the people on either side of me.

"Excusez-moi," I said in my best French accent, straight out of Flushing. All I got in return from the gentleman on my left was a raised eyebrow and that look that said, *You must be an ugly American.* I didn't care, I was at my first Parisian fashion show, all by myself and feeling *très* chic!

The catwalk was decorated to look like a beautiful park. Fresh flowers, trees, and ponds created a feeling of springtime. I had no idea how extravagant fashion shows are. Or how tall and skinny runway models are. I kinda wished I'd skipped the croissant at breakfast, ya know what I mean?

Meanwhile I couldn't believe how ugly a collection this was. See-through everything with combat boots and sticks in the hair. *Oy vey*, there wasn't a thing to buy! Yet as each model entered the stage, the audience broke into a round of applause, coupled with plenty of "oohs" and "ahhs."

"Do you like this?" I nonchalantly asked the lady on my right, pointing to a model wearing a blouse so sheer you could tell she had implants. I mean, nobody that thin has boobs that big.

"Hhmmff," was all she snorted back. And yet that one little grunt transcended any language barriers. I heard her loud and clear. *Don't talk to me, don't even look at me!* it meant, as I meekly began to applaud with everyone else. If you can't beat 'em, join 'em, I always say.

In contrast to that disaster, the couture collection by Yves Saint Laurent was classic, elegant, and gorgeous. The YSL show took place in a small, gilded ballroom of a swanky hotel on the Right Bank.

It was so crowded by the time I arrived, there was hardly a seat to be had. The Frenchman at the door indicated that the doors were closed and no more entry was allowed. *This can't be happening.* I'd had my hair blown out at a salon for this event and there was no way I was going to stand for being turned away. This being my second fashion show, I had a little more chutzpah than for my first. Emphatically, I shook my head and said, "No, no, no," as I charged my way in.

No is *no* in any language, and the next thing I knew I was not only in, but squeezing my chubby ass onto the end of an already crowded bench. I was so happy to have experienced that event. It was so sophisticated and magnificent. All the models looked like Audrey Hepburn as they floated down the runway like something from out of a movie.

Afterward, I met my friend Roxanne at a press party that took place in another room at the same hotel. When I was introduced to one of Saint Laurent's protégés, he looked at the wool pin-striped suit I was wearing and smiled from ear to ear. Clutching my hand, he said, *"Chérie,* I believe you are wearing one of my designs. It is Saint Laurent, no?"

Well, without thinking or taking a beat, I answered, "This? No, it's a Ralph Lauren." In an instant the man's face turned to stone, he dropped my hand and walked away. Wouldn't ya know, when the local news wanted me to answer a few questions, the first one asked was, "Is that suit a Saint Laurent?"

"Yes, yes it is," I replied without hesitation. I'm no fool. . . .

By the time I went to my third show I was already an old hand at this. The Dior men's collection was shown in a building in the Jardin des Plantes, which is a beautiful tree-lined park with a small zoo in it. For this event, Roxanne got me a special V.I.P. pass and I casually waltzed my way to the front of the line, flashed my pass, and entered. Worried that any minute someone was going to tap me on the shoulder and say, "*Au revoir,* Madame, you don't belong here," I tried to act like I was some hotshot magazine editor and no one bothered me.

As I sat down taking in the crowd, I noticed the photographers going nuts over some celebrity, but I couldn't make out who it was. Then with the parting of the waves, I got a clear view of her. I literally rose out of my seat and gazed at, guess who? Catherine Deneuve! I couldn't believe I was finally getting to see her in person. What a gorgeous woman. She wore a stunning black-and-camel suit with dark sunglasses. I bet she speaks a lot of languages, and not just menu, either. She was there with her daughter, who was the image of Marcello Mastroianni. They were laughing and chatting with Karl Lagerfeld, the Chanel designer, with his thick white ponytail and dark glasses. He was waving his famous fan, opening and closing it for emphasis while the paparazzi had a field day.

Watching Catherine and her daughter made me think of my mom. I always miss her when I see mothers and daughters doing nice things together. Mom and I are very close and can always talk about anything. I hope I have a daughter someday so she can grow up feeling she has a mom who's her best friend, too.

This was a men's show, but the models looked like skinny seventeen-year-old waifs. I mean, I like young guys, but this was ridiculous! I don't know how they expected to sell any clothes. It was dramatic, though, when thirty of them marched out all at once dressed in tuxedos.

I met Roxanne backstage where everyone was changing, smoking, kissing, and hugging. One very flamboyant guy ran over to Roxanne with a cigarette in one hand and champagne in the other.

He leaned over and kissed her on each cheek, Euro-style, and then ran off to someone else. Roxanne turned to me all flushed with excitement and said, "He's a prince and always comes to the couture shows."

"Meanwhile, he had a cold sore," I said flatly.

"Oh my God, he did? I didn't even notice," she said, rubbing her mouth.

"Vive la France," I responded, handing her a Wet One from my purse. I was feeling so much better. Paris is one city I have no qualms about visiting on my own, and at this particular time, with the shows in town, everyone was in a real party mode. Festive and gay.

One night my Parisian friends Jean-Pierre—a good-looking independent filmmaker—and his girlfriend, Julie, took me to a really swanky penthouse party. I can't believe I've actually got Parisian friends, let alone invitations to penthouse parties. The apartment was beautiful, with high ceilings and crown moldings. The room was filled with fashionable Parisians, drinking, smoking, and chatting in French. I can't believe how many people still smoke.

I immediately eyeballed the buffet. White-gloved servers stood behind large silver chafing dishes. Ooh-la-la. I was hungry and couldn't wait to dig in. JP and Julie disappeared into the crowd, leaving me to fend for myself. Well, there was a big pile of French bread and a huge bowl of olives calling me over, so I nodded and smiled my way through the crush, drooling at what must be in those chafing dishes.

Curiously, no guests were at the buffet—no one but me, that is. I picked up an olive, popped it in my mouth, grabbed some bread with my left hand, and lifted up the heavy silver dome with my right. But there was nothing inside. Empty. *Bubkes!* The server removed the dome from my hand and said something to me in French that sounded friendly and warm. I didn't want to act like I don't speak the language, so I laughed, nodded, and walked away with a dopey grin pasted on my face. I guess the food wasn't ready yet. But no hors d'oeuvres? My stomach was growling as I champed on my delicious hunk of bread and moved through the crowd in search of JP.

When I finally spotted him, I walked over to say hello. Some of the folks he was talking to spoke English, which was a relief. They all seemed excited to meet me, or rather to meet *La Nounou*, which is French for "the nanny." The show was airing on the M6 network at the time. It's so weird. There I was, unable to say a word in French that didn't fall into the breakfast, lunch, or dinner category, yet they all knew who I was. They asked the same questions people ask everywhere: "Who does your clothes?" "Is that your real voice?" And, "When will you and your boss get together?" I felt happy and included.

The days seemed to fly by. The weather was crisp and clear. Every day I'd walk for miles. It felt so good not to experience the pain anymore.

I was thrilled the day my British friend Simon and his fiancée Anat arrived. I've known Simon for at least fifteen years. And for as long as I'd known him, he'd been single. I mean, Simon was a confirmed bachelor if ever there was one, but then someone introduced him to Anat, and that all changed. As painful as blind dates can be at times, once in a while it does work out. It did for Simon anyway. The first time I met Anat, I liked her right away. Thank goodness. It's always such a pain when someone I've been friends with for years gets involved with someone I just can't stand. Such wasn't the case here, and I really enjoyed spending time with them.

One afternoon, a brisk, sunny day, the three of us walked and talked our way through the Tuileries Gardens. I was missing Chester, and probably boring everyone as I went on and on reminiscing about the trip to Paris I'd taken with him, when the most magical thing happened. Off to the right a small cloud began to drop a column of rain. As the cloud moved, the colorful arc of a rainbow remained. It was a sight to behold. I stood there for several minutes drinking up its beauty as people rushed by, coming and going. I was still reflecting on the rarity of what I was seeing when out of the blue a little kid ran his tricycle right into my shin. "Oww!" I screamed as the kid backed off my foot and pedaled away. But I didn't care; something amazing had just taken place. I'm sure Chester's spirit was connecting with me.

"They say if you speak of the dead and a rainbow appears, it's a sign from your loved one," I said happily to Simon and Anat as I limped away. I felt that my life with Chester finally had closure. This was a good trip for the Franny.

Reunions

After Peter learned of my cancer, we began to correspond through e-mail. It was easier to write letters, and over time the friendship we'd had since high school began to reemerge. It was in late winter, when Peter came to L.A. on business, that we saw each other for the first time in a very long while. He'd e-mailed me and said he'd like to see me if it's what I wanted, too. Well honestly, it's *exactly* what I wanted. In some ways having had cancer wasn't as tough as the total absence of our relationship, our friendship. I thought about how I should look, what I should wear, and what he'd think. I thought about how he'd look, what he'd wear, and what I'd think.

He drove up in a beautiful rented sports car. I felt anxious about it. I wanted it to go well. I opened my front door, pulled him in, and hugged him, and he hugged me back. We embraced for a long time. There were no words, only sighs. Then he complimented me on how young and healthy I looked. To me, he looked like a movie star, not just some ordinary guy. *Dressed cool, good physique, more mature and seasoned,* I thought.

I showed him around the house, a house I'd decorated all by myself (okay, with the help of two decorators and three assistants).

He seemed to like everything. He talked about the movie he'd cowritten and was going to direct, what it was about, and the friends he'd approached to be in it. Danny had generously agreed, as had Twiggy. Rosie was reading the script for the role of the mother. I was so elated to hear how far the project had gone and impressed that he'd made it all happen. He'd become strong for himself without me, and it was lovely to see.

I shut off the volume on my answering machine so we wouldn't be interrupted by phone calls. The first time it rang I didn't think anything of it. Then it rang again and again, at which point I wondered out loud if it was important. What can I say? A ringing phone equals potential emergency in my family. Peter encouraged me to answer it, and then the most amazing thing happened.

"Angel?" It was Rosie on the other end of the line. "Angel, is Peter there? I was talking to your folks and asked them if they knew where I could find him, and they said he was with you!"

"He's right here," I exclaimed.

"Well, put him on, I wanna tell him how much I loved his screenplay and that I'm going to do it!" she added with all the bravura of Pavarotti on stage. It was a miracle. What good news for him to receive, and in my home! What a brilliant, shining moment to share together after so much ugliness. They say coincidence is really God acting anonymously. . . .

"Oh, that's great! Hold on," I said to her, then extended the phone to him, bursting with enthusiasm. "It's Rosie, she loved your screenplay."

His whole face lit up as he took the receiver and did what he as a producer-director does best. He promised Rosie she'd look great, be great, and, above all, be protected by him on all fronts always. I heard him say she could pick whom she wanted to play her husband, which I thought to myself was another smart move.

There was something in the way he paced back and forth in my open living room and kitchen that felt so strangely familiar, so completely the same, as if no time had passed.

When he hung up he gave me a hug, lifting me off the ground and twirling me around. I said something I'm sure I'd said a million times in the past when we'd received good news in our careers: "Let's call Elaine." Suddenly it was him, me, and Elaine again, just like the old days, striving for that break and sometimes catching one. We called my parents and Rosie's agent, too.

Good news always got us hungry, and the next thing you know we were in Peter's sports car taking a long drive up the California coast to a wonderful little Italian restaurant for a late lunch. As the time passed, we shifted into a new gear as effortlessly and seamlessly as a fine-tuned Ferrari. The place was empty as we shared our food and some laughs about the old days. It felt good, a magical moment suspended in time.

The next time we saw each other, it was on Peter's turf, during a business trip I took to New York. It was good to see him in his own environment. I thought he looked great, even better than when I'd seen him in L.A. Not as coiffed as in all our years together, but more rough around the edges, rugged and grungy. It was refreshing to see him being more relaxed in his appearance. I recognized so many things he'd kept that we'd bought together, now part of his beautiful downtown loft. There were the floor lamps that I'd bought for our bedroom so very long ago. He hadn't even liked them when I first brought them home, and there they were, looking beautiful and filled with history and memories.

And it was the first time I met his new puppy, Lumpy. When we were married, he'd never wanted a dog, and so Chester was always more mine than his. I was glad to see he'd gotten one for himself, because now more than ever, I thought how important it was that he experience the unconditional love you can get only from a dog. She was friendly and sweet and high energy—in many ways she reminded me of Chester.

He opened a bottle of my favorite wine and we both toasted to good health as we sat down in his living room. There stood the piano we'd bought used more than twenty years ago during our first year of marriage. We had nothing to our names then, but I couldn't bear the thought of setting up a home without the instrument that enabled him to play such beautiful music. I asked him to play something and sing for me. I hadn't heard Peter sing and play in years, but it was one of my great joys in our relationship.

His voice sounded as strong and powerful as ever, but the song was a sad love song and I began to weep. "Not that one," I interrupted, and he attempted something a bit more lively, but his heart just wasn't in it. We tried a new restaurant called 71 Clinton that neither of us had ever been to before. I thought it would be healthy to create new memories together in new places. We enjoyed it very much, overordered from the menu as always, and found much to laugh about.

As we walked through the streets of the city I marveled at the confidence in his gait and actually questioned him on his obvious lack of fear. "This is where I live," he said confidently. This was a different Peter from the one I'd known in the past. I guess, with the passing of time and circumstance, we'd both matured. He rode with me in the cab back to my hotel and we hugged for a long time before going our separate ways. It was a lovely evening—lovely and bittersweet.

Pet Love

to be able to let go of it all, strip down to nothing, and still feel whole remains my challenge in life. It had never been something I was good at doing, but letting go came easier with the loss of Chester. Whatever wasn't working was given its walking papers. Gone went the lousy aquarium maintenance man. Good-bye, '78 Buick. *Arrivederci* to my agents. The year 2000 was my turning point.

After I'd lit countless candles for Chester, something clicked in my head and I realized that the only way I was going to stop looking back was to start looking forward. I began to refocus my attention from the half-empty glass to its half-full counterpart. Why should I live in my big house without my uterus and without a dog, too? *Who needs all that deprivation at once,* I thought, and began looking for a puppy. My therapist always used to remind me that "being alone" and "loneliness" needn't go hand in hand.

I worried that I'd never bond with a new puppy the way I had with Chester, but I definitely needed a new distraction, no matter what. I couldn't decide what breed I wanted, but I kinda thought a female would be nice this time around. Years of Chester's lifting his leg on my curtains convinced me of that! I surfed the Internet for breeders and visited many pet stores on the west side of L.A. All the puppies were adorable, but none sparked the connection I felt when I first laid eyes on Chester. I must say, though, that as a way of putting the mourning period completely behind me, my search was very effective. More than anything, it was an exciting diversion.

I bought a dog book with four hundred different breeds, and slowly began to narrow my choices. At first I thought of getting a big dog, but when I thought of how much exercise a big dog needs—not to mention the size of its pees and shits—I changed my mind. I was thinking a white or tan dog would look nice in my house, but on the other hand, I usually wear black, and who needs white fur all over black clothes?

So I decided I wanted a female that didn't shed. Small was better—it'd be more like having a baby. And now that I had a clue what I wanted, it was easier entering a pet shop.

Cousin Erica, who's a costumer and spends a lot of time shopping in malls, said that Pet Love in the Beverly Center offered a big selection of really cute dogs. I remembered Danny and Donna got their first Akita there, and Elaine and Allan found both their Lhasa apsos there, too. They loved their dogs and they all lived long and healthy lives.

Before I became famous, Judi, Peter, and I had spent more time in that mall than I care to remember. Between the multiplex cinemas, the food court, the shops, and the pet store we could easily spend half a day in that place. But for the last several years it had been difficult moving about freely without getting stopped for autographs, so big shopping malls were off-limits. As John and I charged through the arcade of shops on the plaza level heading for Pet Love, I took it all in. So much activity, so much to look at, and so many new stores!

When we entered Pet Love it was overwhelming: the size of

the shop and the selection of dogs. The place was filled with cus-
tomers. I would have sworn it was Christmastime, given the size
of the crowds and the store's busy feel. Our salesperson was very
patient and understanding. This isn't an easy decision to make for
anyone, and I'm a person who has trouble deciding what to order
in a restaurant, so you can only imagine. They put us in a private
little stall, complete with toys and paper towels, and brought in
each puppy we were considering.

I read somewhere that it's a good idea when seriously considering a puppy to observe how it interacts with its peers. That way,
you can gauge how playful, timid, or aggressive it may be. One little pup immediately began humping another and I said, "Take
him away." If that's starting at *this* age, forget about it. Not for me.
John liked a white male Pom that was really cute and very playful.
Too playful, if you asked me. This was a Chester Drescher waiting
to happen, and in this go-round I didn't want hyper.

I noticed an ultrafeminine, quiet, brown little Pom sitting by
herself and asked to see her. I'd never seen a chocolate Pom—she
was the first they'd ever had at the pet store. She was very quiet
and serene. Not particularly interactive, but not timid, either. She
was a perfect little lady and I was drawn to her. She didn't seem
puppylike, but regal and elegant. John kept having them bring in
one puppy after another, but, oh, that precious little brown one.

Then suddenly the words left my mouth: "She's the one," and
the salesgirl immediately shifted into accessory mode. *Did I just
say what I thought I said?* I began to shut down as tiny rhinestoned
collars and leopard-print leashes were waved in my face. Seconds
after leaving the pen, the brown puppy peed and shit on the pet
shop floor as the gal whisked her off for fluffing, and I began to
think of the new white carpet I'd installed in my bedroom after
Chester died.

I suddenly felt so weak in the knees, I had to sit down. What was I doing? Who was this strange, aloof little brown dog and what kind of a friend would she be to me? Then I began to think about what an enormous commitment this was. These dogs live to at least fifteen. My God, I'll be pushing sixty. *Oy,* I began to have a panic attack, but forged ahead anyway.

On the car ride home I cradled the tiny brown creature with huge sad eyes and a spindly little pencil neck. My maternal instincts began to kick in as I felt a powerful need to make her feel safe. I had a baby. Poor little thing, taken from her real mama, shipped to Pet Love only two days earlier, and now uprooted once again. Everyone was a stranger, everything was so unfamiliar to my sweet little girl.

"Esther!" I blurted out.

"Esther?" John questioned.

"Yes, after my great-grandmother. It's a wonderful ancient name," I added.

Esther was the distraction I needed. Not a replacement, but an addition. Esther is all about today and tomorrow—not about yesterday—and that's what makes her so vital for my emotional recovery. She's her own little being, though, nothing like the little ham that Chester was. He loved the camera and all the show-biz action. I'd always bring him along to photo shoots and sure enough, before the day was done, that little guy was smiling for the camera and joining me on a magazine cover. I mean, that dog had his own Web site and fan club! Would Esther love my world as much? Could I maintain the same fun "celebrity and her doggie" persona, or were those days gone forever?

When I got an offer to do a commercial, my first "real" job since the cancer, it seemed simple enough and I decided to accept. I thought it would be a good reentry to the biz.

In the commercial I'm a celebrity at a photo shoot talking about my new handheld digital organizer, and I thought it might be fun to include Esther in the spot. So I brought my girl and pow-wowed with the producers, the agency people, and the director, Larry, whom I'd worked with before.

I had an idea that it would be great eye candy if I kept changing throughout the thirty-second spot. I'm known for my fashion sense and I thought it supported the celebrity photo shoot concept. So Shawn-Holly, who'd costumed *The Nanny* for years, spread out our selections. Old habits die hard, I guess. All those years producing *The Nanny* had trained me to think on my feet, and this time was no different. They bought my concept hook, line, and sinker. I'd change three times and include little Esther in the commercial. I remember asking the prop man to glue the teacup to the saucer because each time it was handed over on camera, it rattled. Always a stickler for details, I also requested a lipstick print be made on the edge of the cup for realism. Of course, I wanted someone else to make the lip print since there was no way I was going to screw up the beautiful lip job my makeup man Gregory had done.

It all went like clockwork. Esther, looking adorable, appeared at the top of the spot before I passed her off to an actor playing my assistant. I felt like a real backstage mother pushing her into the limelight to follow in the paw prints of her older, dead brother. But hey, this was my life and she better get used to it. Faye, who also did my hair on *The Nanny,* combed me and Esther out beautifully as Elaine watched the monitors along with the agency executives.

That same day I shot a public service announcement for the Gynecologic Cancer Foundation, *sans* Esther, which also went very well. I rewrote the copy (of course) to express in greater detail how urgent it is to take the necessary tests to diagnose cancer at its early stages. I gave the Web site for women's cancer: www.wcn.org. It was poetic shooting the two jobs back to back, because each represented a huge factor in my life: my career and my cancer.

And so it went. My life was taking on a new shape, piece by piece, little by little. I had my health back, I was beginning to work again, and the dog, especially the dog, made a world of difference. It broke my heart the day I had to get Esther fixed. Bob Barker always ends *The Price Is Right* by telling his audience to "get your pets spayed or neutered," and I figured he must know best. So we brought Esther to get the very same surgery I had. I hated to put her through it, even though we were told it was better for her long-term overall health.

Would the change throw off her hormones? Would she go into a surgical menopause? The vet said no on all fronts. *But do they really know?* I wondered. In the end I guess you gotta trust someone, so we had it done. The vet said after about a week she'd be completely her old self, but it really took several weeks. Sound familiar?

One Year Later

It had been explained to me by my surgeon that when you've been diagnosed and treated for cancer, you can't consider yourself cured or out of the woods until you've had five years of nonrecurrence. So with each month that passed and each good report, my chances of recurrence diminished as the odds began to stack more and more in my favor.

It was daunting, knowing I'd have to be tested by the surgeon every three months for the first two years and then every six months for three years after that. I couldn't believe I'd have to continue returning to that hospital for the next five years!

But I'd been told over and over again that consistency of follow-up is the most essential factor in long-term recovery. Doctor #9 couldn't stress enough the importance: "Women who find themselves too busy to do their follow-up are basically giving up, since they've left the race when it's only been half run."

John, bless his heart, had come with me to every post-op checkup. I felt strong and healthy, but as each three-month cycle came to an end I worried the surgeon might say something I didn't want to hear. Each hospital visit was a vivid reminder of the horror of it all. But the one-year checkup had greater significance. At the one-year point, they do a CT (pronounced "cat") scan and see exactly what's going on inside. This is the time when they look for new growths.

John and I entered the hospital just as we had so many times in the past year. Immediately, I began to feel clammy and weak. *Am I still cancer-free?* John stayed with me in the examining room, too. My surgeon performed the physical exam. I'd thought I'd be taking the scan that same day, but no mention was made of it until me and my big mouth brought it up. Then Doctor #9 remembered it was my one-year anniversary. Of course, that a whole year had passed since my cancer surgery couldn't have had the same resonance for her as for me.

I didn't even know what a CT scan was, exactly, so she explained that the letters stood for "computerized tomography" and that the machine would take a series of X rays showing thin slices of my body from front to back, starting at my thigh and going up my neck.

"Why do they have to go all the way up to the neck?" I asked.

"Because sometimes recurrence can show up in the lungs," she answered. Well, if that didn't make me nauseous.

The next morning, I made an appointment with the nurse but was very apprehensive. I worried about having to take more X rays. I mean, maybe the effects of all those X rays would somehow accumulate and ignite any cancer cells that might be lying dormant. What if I'd never even brought up the scan? Was this absolutely necessary?

When I spoke to my friend Melinda, she told me she'd never had to have a CT scan and had just celebrated her second year of postsurgery nonrecurrence. So of course, I called Doctor #9's nurse and questioned her about all this. I'm sure doctors and nurses hate when patients know each other and compare notes, but who cares? I wanted to know why I needed a CT scan and Melinda didn't.

"Everyone's different," I was told. "You don't have to take it this week if you don't want to, but you *will* have to take it," the nurse reasoned. No point in postponing, I figured, and grudgingly kept the appointment.

I've heard there's a lot of controversy about these CT scans. Healthy people plunk down a lot of cash just to take a look-see around. Everyone's heard the story of the guy who felt perfectly fine and took a CT scan that detected a spot on his liver: an early detection that saved his life. But Elaine's doctor told her there can be dozens of cysts and nodes and lumps throughout our bodies, most of which are totally benign. "Why look for trouble?" was his philosophy.

Rachel had a CT done on her lungs. She's a mother of two, and after years of smoking she thought she'd sleep better knowing her lungs were clean. It was a relief to learn they were. Who knows whether it's a good preventive measure or just "looking for trouble"? I was about to find out for myself.

The next day when John and I arrived, a technician asked me to drink something that helps enhance the CT images. I got to mix it with the beverage of my choice and chose iced tea, downing two large glasses full. Next, I was led to an area where I changed into a hospital gown. Sue, a nurse who doesn't normally work in this area, had been called down to help out. After several unsuccessful attempts, she finally managed to put an I.V. into the vein in my hand. Even though John thought I was overreacting, it hurt like hell.

Then the nurse disappeared and a big, Nordic-looking, very pretty technician led me over to the CT scan machine. John was able to sit behind glass in a separate room and watch. The technician hooked up my I.V. to a dye, which hurt going into my veins. When she reduced the pressure the pain receded.

The first thing she said was, "Why did they put the I.V. in your *hand?*" As if I knew why.

"What's the matter? Is that bad?" I questioned nervously.

"Well, they usually do the top of the hand with old people, but I don't know why she'd do this to you." Not exactly confidence-building words to hear as you're placed in a huge contraption and pumped full of a strange dye. "Who did this?" she wondered.

"Sue, it was Sue!" I accused. "Does it make any difference?" I continued, wanting in that moment to stab Sue.

"It's just that your arms need to be out of the way, and with the I.V. in your hand it's harder to lift your arms over your head," the Nordic nurse replied.

"Stupid Sue," I muttered as the technician disappeared behind the glass. And the scan began! Aside from a slight nervousness caused by having a large instrument looming over you, the scan itself is nothing with nothing. Even less so if you're fortunate enough not to get Sue.

By the time it was over and I began to get dressed, I noticed that the hand that had been repeatedly jabbed by Sue was already swollen and turning black and blue. So I marched myself back into the technician's area, where the Nordic nurse was already kibitzing with one of the doctors. As I approached, flailing my purple, swollen hand, I shouted, *"Sue, Sue!"*

"Oh, we don't like to use that word around here," the doctor replied, getting nervous. But the pretty Nordic nurse explained that Sue was the gal who'd inserted the I.V., and together she and the doctor assured me that although my hand would stay quite ugly for several days, eventually the bruising would fade.

"Why me, Lord?" I whimpered, heading for the nearest antiques store to appease my aggravation.

Well, that was on Thursday, and it wasn't until Tuesday that Wanda, my surgeon's nurse, called with the test results.

"I have good news and not-so-good news," she said, "but we don't really think it's anything bad and we're not worried, or Doctor #9 would have called you herself."

Had she just said what I thought she said? I looked over at John, who knew something was up, and meekly replied, "Is something wrong, did something show up on the CT scan?"

"Your abdomen is completely clean," Wanda assured, "and that's very important, because that's the first and most likely area spread would occur."

I gulped. "So what's the not-so-good part?" I asked, as my voice weakened and John ran to pick up an extension.

"They found a spot on your lung," she said, forthright and direct as always (they must take a class for that). She then quickly added, "But nothing about the spot looks suspicious in any way. Many people have small growths on their lungs from birth, and they're not threatening at all. It's smooth like a river rock that has been there for many years, and doesn't look anything like cancer, which is jagged with tentacles. Still, considering your recent history, Doctor #9 thinks we should do a PET scan just to be sure." She assured me that if I hadn't been a recovering cancer patient, they'd never have pursued this further.

I understood the words she was saying, but my heart sank as my fears rose. "Wait a minute, what did the CT scan do, and what the hell is a PET scan for?" I asked. *And why do they all sound like domesticated animals?*

Wanda was ready with all the answers: "The CT scan detects a growth; a PET scan determines whether or not it's malignant. Theoretically, any malignancies you have will grab at sugar, so they inject you with a radioactive sugar fluid that appears as highlights in the PET scan pictures." Uh-huh. It was all so futuristic I couldn't even believe what I was hearing.

"Well, why didn't this spot show up on those stupid chest X rays I took before my surgery?" I questioned.

"Because it's hidden behind a bone," she said matter-of-factly. "It wouldn't have been visible with a simple chest X ray. An appointment for a PET scan should be set as soon as possible. Call Doctor #9's scheduling nurse in the morning to confirm," Wanda instructed.

I hung up the phone so sad and upset. I wasn't prepared to feel this way again. But in a repeat performance, I immediately began dialing my parents, sister, and friends.

The next morning when I called the gal in my surgeon's office, she said she was waiting to hear from the people over at Nuclear Medicine and hoping to work something out over the next few weeks.

"Few weeks!" I exclaimed. Here I was, thinking I'd be going in that afternoon or the next day at the very latest. I mean, how do they expect you to get on with your life when you know you've got a phantom spot on your lung? "Gimme the number, let me talk to them," I said, offering to lend a helping hand.

When I called, I got a guy named Tom on the phone who said the department was really backed up with appointments. But when I told him I'd had uterine cancer and that my CT scan showed a spot on my lung, my voice began quivering out of control. He asked how late I could come in that same day and I said, "Whenever you say, Tom."

Then he asked if I'd eaten, and I said no. I knew not to eat or drink anything until I found out when my test was going to be and what restrictions it might require. He said he'd see what he could do and call me right back.

Within minutes he phoned back and said they'd make me the last appointment of the day. I blessed him and thanked him profusely. He suggested I eat some pure protein—chicken or fish—right away, then nothing but water until after the test.

As I hung up, relieved but anxious about what lay ahead, Ramon asked, "Fran, have you ever jumped out of a plane with a parachute?"

Tearfully I said, "No, Ramon, I never went skydiving. I'm not a thrill seeker in that way." And then I really began to bawl. He quickly realized this wasn't the time to talk about daredevil sports.

"What's the matter, something wrong?" he asked gently.

I could barely get the words out as I said, "My test didn't come back so good. The doctors need me to take more. I have to go today."

Ramon put down his mop and said to me, as if he really knew, "Fran, there is nothing wrong with you. I can tell in your eyes, you are healthy!" Then he picked up the mop and walked away. Softly, I said, "Thank you, Ramon."

Both Elaine and Rachel said they wanted to be with me for the PET scan. Wednesday at four-thirty was the time; Nuclear Medicine was the place. John would arrive a bit later after a meeting he had. Camelia would pick me up and drive me to the hospital. Kathy would stay with Esther.

I must say, I was blessed to find myself surrounded by all these very wise and loving women. Each had known what it was to live life, as well as to feel pain and heartache. With them I can speak freely about hormones, cancer, and growing older. Without inhibition or embarrassment I can talk about my estrogen patch, gray hair, or wrinkles. They helped ease me into my new reality as painlessly and shamelessly as possible, pointing out the bumps in the road so I might fall fewer times and trip less. More and more I believe in a master plan and the subtle maneuvers from the angels above.

When Camelia came to pick me up for the PET scan, I kept procrastinating. I didn't want to go back to the hospital. I was afraid to take that test, afraid of what it might tell me. So while she sat with her car keys in hand, waiting, I felt the sudden need to prepare Kathryn a big bowl of spaghetti. I didn't want to believe this was anything more than a false alarm, but a tiny voice inside me feared the worst. I remember thinking, *Is this how it's going to be for me? Intermittent blocks of remission followed by one cancer after another?*

When we finally arrived at the hospital, the two of us navigated our way through the corridors to the dreaded door marked NUCLEAR MEDICINE. I was so grateful to Tom for squeezing me in that I'd brought him a box of chocolates. When Elaine and Rachel arrived, the whole atmosphere of the waiting room lifted. In two minutes we'd taken over and rearranged the whole lobby. Everyone was thirsty and I immediately began doling out cups from the water cooler. Always the hostess with the mostess.

Rachel helped me fill out the forms. It's so weird checking off the YES box for cancer, hysterectomy, appendectomy, and thyroiditis. I looked at her and said, "Can you believe this is me?" One of the questions they asked was whether I might be pregnant. My answer was no. By the time we got down to COMMENTS, all I could write was "Tom is nice."

It was Tom who took me to get the injection of the radioactive sugar solution. Rachel came along for support and also to use the bathroom. The framed posters, paintings, and photographs that lined the walls were the only memorable landmarks in a maze of otherwise nondescript hallways and doors. Both she and I made a pit stop at what Tom described as the "cleaner" bathroom, and then continued on to the room where I'd get my injection.

Tom said that I'd have to wait at least another thirty minutes to allow the stuff to spread throughout my body. I jokingly said I was going to start a rock band and call it "Radioactive Girl."

He also explained that a PET scan is particularly effective at photographing the lungs, since they normally won't take in the sugar at all. So Rachel and I returned to the waiting room, where Elaine sat knitting and chatting with Camelia.

Finally, at around 6 P.M., they led me in for the PET scan. The room itself was on the small side, and they felt only one person should sit with me in there. The rest of the brood sat just outside the curtain in the hallway, well within earshot.

Elaine sat with me initially and gabbed about her grandchildren while continuing to knit. She was a comforting presence as I hung on every word about little Ruby, the latest addition to the family. When John finally arrived, he took over for Elaine and filled me in on his meeting.

Through the curtain that divided us from Elaine, Rachel, and Camelia we collectively discussed where we should eat when this was done. After an hour of taking the photos, I got dressed and we all walked over to Ubon, a Japanese noodle house. I kept my cell phone on as I waited for the call from my surgeon, who promised to give me an initial evaluation of the PET scan from the head doctor of Nuclear Medicine.

There we all were, drinking sake and digging our chopsticks into noodles and sushi, when the phone rang. We all froze. I flipped open the receiver as everyone looked on. Doctor #9 was so great about calling as quickly as she did. It was eight o'clock at night, and she was still making calls on my behalf. I wondered how many hours out of each day she actually devoted to her private life, but was grateful for her commitment to her patients.

The first thing she said was, "There's no sign of cancer anywhere," and I instantly gave everyone at the table the thumbs-up. In the morning she said she'd have a team of pulmonary (lung) specialists also look at the film, but that I should relax and enjoy my dinner.

When I hung up the phone, John, teary-eyed, thanked me for

putting my thumb up so as not to prolong their agony. The first thing Elaine said was, "Call your folks and we'll hear whatever you tell them!"

My mom had been extremely anxious all day over this whole thing. Each time we spoke she'd answer the phone before the first ring finished, and this time was no different. It was 11 P.M. in Florida. "Yeah, hello," she answered, sounding a bit frantic—and rightfully so.

"It's definitely not cancer, there's no sign of cancer anywhere!" I said, rushing to get all the words out.

"Our prayers have been answered, that's all we wish for, that you should be well," my mom exclaimed. She sent her love to everyone, told us to enjoy our dinner, and added, "Now we can go to sleep." I was all aglow, both figuratively and literally. I raised my sake cup to my hero and heroines, and thanked them for their unending love and support.

Alone, but Not Lonely

October 2001

baseball play-offs were in full swing and John, along with some buddies of his, drove to San Francisco for the big Yankees versus Oakland A's games. I, on the other hand, had been trying to finish this book all week, but had been distracted by re-modeling questions and plans for my November New York trip, so I was really looking forward to being left alone to catch up on the writing. It's the rare occasion when the house is empty and quiet.

By Friday afternoon everyone was gone for the weekend. No hammering and banging coming from the upstairs, no housekeepers, no assistants, no nothing. Just me and Esther and the gentle sounds of ocean waves. I love the way the house looks when it's all clean. White flowers in vases everywhere, shiny waxed floors, fresh towels, and crisp linens on the bed. There's a serenity to my home. It's a truly special place and I cherish those peaceful moments when I can enjoy it on my own.

I knew that I needed an ending to the book. But how do you end a story about having cancer when you still have four more years of checkups to go? Every time I'd write something it became a chapter, but not the last chapter. I'd been racking my brain over this for weeks, knowing full well my deadline was fast approaching, but had no luck coming up with anything. This was to be the weekend, like it or not.

When I awoke on Saturday morning, I opened my bedroom door to gaze upon one of my favorite views in the house. As the sun sifted through the sheer curtains of my dining room, it cast a soft light on the table and the hydrangeas in my Lalique vase that has female nudes around it. The angel statues that stand atop my sideboard were also beautifully lit and especially ethereal looking.

Esther awakened and greeted the rest of the house with me. I decided to not get dressed at all that day, but rather to walk freely about my home nude. Together, we went out on my deck and took in the stillness of the early-morning hour. The fog was thick and the ocean hardly visible. While Esther sniffed around, making her first discoveries of the day, I stretched toward the sky and inhaled the salt air. I decided not to answer the phones, but focus solely on writing the last chapter.

I reentered the house and went into my bath area. I love this room so much. I'd hung a magnificent chandelier from the center of the skylight. There's an aquarium in this room that adds so much greenery and quiet beauty. I find the fish tranquil as they gracefully swim through the leaves. I changed my estrogen patch. I'm on a Saturday/Wednesday schedule. I don't take the daily pill because I can't get it in the amount that makes me feel the best (even-tempered), so I wear a patch and then cut a second patch into quarters, which gives me the perfect amount, and change it twice a week.

Melinda takes the pill version of the hormone replacement patch, but she feels good on one of the standard doses. I don't. They advise you to switch the spot where you place the patch each time you change it. I removed it from my left hip and put the new patch and a quarter on my right. I've found that eye-makeup remover gets off any residue adhesive from the old side, so I swabbed the area with a moistened cotton pad.

I was trying to get back into shape, anticipating the upcoming trip to New York where I'd be honored with the Gilda Award at the Gilda's Club Seventh Annual Comedy Gala fund-raiser. It seemed fitting I accept the honor since I'd spent so much time thinking about Gilda Radner during my search for a diagnosis. The award committee had chosen me the celebrity cancer survivor of the year. Hard to fathom, but nevertheless true.

As I walked past my mirrored closet doors I took in the shape of my body and I liked what I saw. My butt looked firm, my tummy looked flat, the exercise and dieting seemed to be paying off. I saw the little patch and a quarter pasted to my hip, but it didn't bother me anymore. I remembered how in the beginning I'd cried to John about how much I hated it. It seemed like a brand to me, a reminder I had cancer. I didn't want it on me, nor did I want the scar where they'd made the incision. Now the scar's hardly noticeable, and the patch seems more like a medal for bravery.

It's great being home alone. I never thought the day would come when I'd say that and mean it, but I do. I looked down at Esther and said to her, "Everyone loves you, but I get to keep you all of the time!" She's just the dearest, sweetest thing, and I adore her. Getting another dog was definitely the right thing to do.

John called to let me know he arrived safely. I told him I planned to walk around the house naked all day. I love to be nude; it makes me feel so free. He said, "Take Esther's collar off so she can be naked, too. She always likes it when the collar is off and she gets her neck scratched." He's a thoughtful "Poppy" and it fills my heart to witness how caring and tender he is with her. So I took off her collar and she did seem to be freer and lighter.

I no longer feel anxiety or any kind of weight on my shoulders. It comes as a great relief that I've arrived at this place in my life. I walked through fire to confront my fears, and thank God, it wasn't in vain. I now know who I am. I'm comfortable by myself. And that makes all the difference.

Now I'm a new person with a new man, a new dog, a new house, and a new life. There's so much good that's come out of the cancer. I feel such compassion for others' pain. I have deeper friendships and more meaningful bonds with my parents, my sister, and John. I've formed new relationships I otherwise might never have had, and renewed old ones that might have remained estranged.

As I toasted a bagel and poured a mug of green tea, Esther ate her kibble. I then retreated to my rocker with my legal pad and pen. And as the waves crashed against the shoreline and the morning sun began to burn off the fog, I wondered how I could write the last chapter.

That's when I realized I just did.

"Hope" is the thing with feathers—
That perches in the soul—
And sings the tunes without the words—
And never stops—at all—

—Emily Dickinson